D1623093

PRAISE FOR
THE POWER OF PLACE

"I can't recommend *The Power of Place* highly enough. Everyone needs to read it! It is beautifully written, compellingly argued, and urgently necessary for a rootless generation like our own. I particularly appreciate the way Daniel Grothe has earthed his message practically in the rich loam of friendships and the home. This book sits squarely in the tradition of the Greats, from Benedict of Nursia in Umbria to Wendell Berry of Henry County in Kentucky. As for Daniel Grothe, I consider him one of the most brilliant pastors of generation, arising as a thinker and writer of rare talent."

—PETE GREIG, FOUNDER OF 24-7 PRAYER INTERNATIONAL,
SENIOR PASTOR OF EMMAUS RD, AND AUTHOR OF *HOW TO PRAY*

difficult to overstate the importance of this message for culture right now. The nearly ubiquitous, frayed edges of our reveal that we are a profoundly uprooted people. With great and pastoral care, Daniel Grothe puts his finger on the sickness that ails us. My sincere hope is that Christians read this with the urgency it warrants."

—SHARON HODDE MILLER, AUTHOR OF *FREE OF ME:
WHY LIFE IS BETTER WHEN IT'S NOT ABOUT YOU*

"We settled into spaces given to us by God and those spaces are good. This book will help all of us put down crucial roots in the soil of our neighborhoods, our cities, and our churches. Pastor Daniel Grothe takes us on a beautiful journey to discover the power of place and the fruit that's produced by remaining."

—BRADY BOYD, SENIOR PASTOR OF NEW LIFE CHURCH

"Daniel Grothe is one of my favorite pastors. He carries in him a spirit of deep wisdom, helping us pay attention to the reality of God's presence right where we are. In this much needed book, Daniel offers a vision of *stability* for a world increasingly marked by distraction, transience, and rootless technological omnipresence. We were made to be present—to God, to each other, and to the rest of creation—and Daniel shows us how to do this through his life and a beautiful exploration of the Scriptures. As a pastor in a busy city, I desperately need this book to help me remain fully present to the gifts already before me."

—RICH VILLODAS, LEAD PASTOR OF NEW LIFE FELLOWSHIP
AND AUTHOR OF *THE DEEPLY FORMED LIFE*

"The vow of stability and the life it creates are an appealing antidote to the restless longing of our age. But even more compelling is the man who invites us into it. I've known Daniel Grothe for over two decades, and I am proud to call him both a friend and a colleague. This book is not a collection of concepts harvested from other fields. It is filled with lessons that have come with scars and a calling that has been cultivated with intentionality and sacrifice. Grounded in theology and buttressed by the wisdom of Christian history, the principles and practices in the pages have the power to form deep roots for your soul and the life of the world."

—GLENN PACKIAM, LEAD PASTOR OF NEW LIFE DOWNTOWN
AND AUTHOR OF *BLESSED BROKEN G[...]*

"We live in a digital age where so little of our life feels ro[...] anything physical, things we can touch with our fingers [...] with our toes. We also live in an ambitious age where all [...] ety's energy prods us to move as fast as we can, as far as [...] can. Yet, amid all this, here's Daniel Grothe with the audacit[...] sug- gest that it is often more courageous (and more human) to[...] tight, stay slow, and go deep. Leave it to someone with a pastor's heart and a poet's pen to wake us up and provoke us toward goodness. If Daniel's got the courage to tell us the truth, then I hope we'll have the courage to listen."

—WINN COLLIER, PASTOR, AUTHOR OF *LOVE BIG, BE WELL*
AND *A BURNING IN MY BONES*, AND DIRECTOR OF THE
EUGENE PETERSON CENTER FOR CHRISTIAN IMAGINATION

"Centuries ago, one of the great luminaries of the Egyptian desert, St. Anthony the Great, gave a simple (and demanding) road map to holiness when he said, 'Whoever you may be, always have God before your eyes; whatever you do, do it according to the testimony of the holy Scriptures; *in whatever place you live, do not easily leave it.*' Human lives require stable contexts in order to flourish, which is why the ancient vow of stability is so important. Sadly, our culture has reversed this ancient wisdom, teaching us to see stability as at least a nuisance and at most a deep danger to the path of self-actualization. To the extent that we believe this, we are unwitting co-conspirators in the diminishment of our lives.

It is time and past time that we take back our lives by recovering the ancient wisdom of stability. To do this, we'll need wise guides schooled in the fine art of stability to help us. Daniel Grothe is one such guide. He is well qualified by training and experience to lead us into the picture painted by the psalmist: 'That person is like a tree planted by streams of water, which yields its fruit in season and whose leaf does not wither—whatever they do prospers' (Psalm 1:3). Well written and well argued, and packed with brilliant examples (ancient and modern) of what the vow of stability looks like in practice, *The Power of Place* is a book for our time."

—ANDREW ARNDT, LEAD PASTOR OF NEW LIFE EAST
AND AUTHOR OF *ALL FLAME*

"Eugene Peterson once remarked, 'All theology is rooted in geography.' I didn't fully understand the weight behind those six words until I read this book. We are living in an age when jumping after bigger opportunities, platforms, and paychecks has become the norm. It's even confused today as God's favor. I'm grateful for how Daniel Grothe guides and reminds us that staying put in a specific city can actually produce a more deeply meaningful life in us and through us. *The Power of Place* is an essential read for anyone like me who struggles with wanderlust, or for anyone who believes the grass is always greener somewhere else. This book will help you discover the redemptive potential of where God has planted you!"

—STEVE CARTER, PASTOR AND AUTHOR OF
THE THING BENEATH THE THING

"We live in a restless age obsessed with living our best possible life, and this has led to a profound disconnectedness and angst. Daniel Grothe gets to the heart of this angst by calling us to a deep rootedness that satisfies our souls. He invites us to deepen our sense of place, marriage, friendship, and spiritual community in a beautiful vision that calls us back to a better way. I'm grateful for Daniel's voice. It is a voice forged from some hard-earned wisdom."

—STEVE CUSS, AUTHOR OF
MANAGING LEADERSHIP ANXIETY

THE POWER OF PLACE

Choosing Stability in a Rootless Age

DANIEL GROTHE

NELSON
BOOKS

An Imprint of Thomas Nelson

Published in Nashville, Tennessee, by Nelson Books, an imprint of Thomas Nelson. Nelson Books and Thomas Nelson are registered trademarks of HarperCollins Christian Publishing, Inc.

Published in association with The Bindery Agency, www.TheBinderyAgency.com.

Thomas Nelson titles may be purchased in bulk for educational, business, fundraising, or sales promotional use. For information, please e-mail SpecialMarkets@ThomasNelson.com.

Unless otherwise noted, Scripture quotations taken from The Holy Bible, New International Version®, NIV®. Copyright © 1973, 1978, 1984, 2011 by Biblica, Inc.® Used by permission of Zondervan. All rights reserved worldwide. www.Zondervan.com. The "NIV" and "New International Version" are trademarks registered in the United States Patent and Trademark Office by Biblica, Inc.®

Scripture quotations marked ESV are taken from the ESV® Bible (The Holy Bible, English Standard Version®). Copyright © 2001 by Crossway, a publishing ministry of Good News Publishers. Used by permission. All rights reserved.

Scripture quotations marked KJV are taken from the King James Version. Public domain.

Scripture quotations marked THE MESSAGE are taken from *THE MESSAGE*. Copyright © 1993, 2002, 2018 by Eugene H. Peterson. Used by permission of NavPress. All rights reserved. Represented by Tyndale House Publishers, Inc.

The Scripture quotations marked NRSV are taken from the New Revised Standard Version Bible. Copyright © 1989 National Council of the Churches of Christ in the United States of America. Used by permission. All rights reserved worldwide.

Any internet addresses, phone numbers, or company or product information printed in this book are offered as a resource and are not intended in any way to be or to imply an endorsement by Thomas Nelson, nor does Thomas Nelson vouch for the existence, content, or services of these sites, phone numbers, companies, or products beyond the life of this book.

ISBN: 978-1-4002-1258-3 (Audiobook)

Library of Congress Cataloging-in-Publication Data

Names: Grothe, Daniel, 1982- author.
Title: The power of place : choosing stability in a rootless age / Daniel Grothe.
Description: Nashville, Tennessee : Thomas Nelson, [2021] | Includes bibliographical references. | Summary: "Acclaimed teaching pastor Daniel Grothe speaks to the sense of loneliness that many feel in today's age of hypermobility and noncommittal wandering, reminding us of the ancient vow of stability and teaching us how we can lead a richer life of friendship, community, and purpose"-- Provided by publisher.
Identifiers: LCCN 2021005173 (print) | LCCN 2021005174 (ebook) | ISBN 9781400212538 (hardcover) | ISBN 9781400212545 (epub)
Subjects: LCSH: Church membership. | Church attendance. | Communities--Religious aspects--Christianity. | Choice of church. | Change--Religious aspects--Christianity.
Classification: LCC BV4525 .G76 2021 (print) | LCC BV4525 (ebook) | DDC 254/.5--dc23
LC record available at https://lccn.loc.gov/2021005173
LC ebook record available at https://lccn.loc.gov/2021005174

Printed in the United States of America

21 22 23 24 25 LSC 10 9 8 7 6 5 4 3 2 1

For Daniel Kemp Wilson and
Louise "Weezie" Wilson,
my maternal grandparents, who helped
teach me the love of place.

CONTENTS

PART I: THE *POWER* OF STABILITY IN PLACE

Chapter 1 Wanderlust: *Why We Feel the Pull to Leave* 3

Chapter 2 The Vow of Stability: *Why We Don't Need a New Place to Have a Rich Life* 21

Chapter 3 The Gift of Place: *A New Perspective on Belonging* 41

PART II: THE *PRINCIPLES* OF STABILITY IN PLACE

Chapter 4 Honoring Your Location: *The Membership Benefits of Place* 57

Chapter 5 Honoring Your Relationships: *People Are the Great Purifiers* 79

Chapter 6 Honoring Your Service: *What Your Skills Can Do* 89

Chapter 7 Honoring Your Presence: *Everywhere You Are Is Sacred* 105

PART III: THE *PRACTICES* OF STABILITY IN PLACE

A Brief Interlude: *We Need Holy Practices* 125

Chapter 8   Stability in Home 129
Chapter 9   Stability in Family 139
Chapter 10   Stability in Friendship 159
Chapter 11   Stability in Church 175
Chapter 12   Stability in Community 191
Chapter 13   A Sacred Stay 199

Afterword: *When You Can't Stay* 207
Acknowledgments 217
Notes 219
About the Author 229

PART I

THE *POWER* OF STABILITY IN PLACE

CHAPTER 1

WANDERLUST

Why We Feel the Pull to Leave

That person is like a tree planted by streams
of water,
which yields its fruit in season
and whose leaf does not wither—
whatever they do prospers.
—*Psalm 1:3*

THE EMAIL CAME OUT OF NOWHERE. A SEARCH firm representing one of the largest churches in America reached out to me unexpectedly. The church had lost their senior pastor to a very public and scandalous series of infidelities and indiscretions. He was a legend in American evangelicalism (a status that anyone should be deathly afraid of) and had fashioned himself as a leadership guru (which always seems to be a part of the forecast leading up to a failure). It turned out he was living a lie. He was gone overnight, and now the church was unraveling.

Our congregation had gone through a similar crisis and lost our founding pastor more than a decade before. In the aftermath of our own unraveling, I had learned some things alongside my colleagues about caring for a church in crisis. Now the search firm wanted to know if I wanted to put that learning to work. Without my knowing, some folks had recommended me to them. Would I consider a conversation on becoming their new senior pastor?

The conversation was unexpected for at least a couple of reasons. First, I hadn't applied for the job. I didn't know anyone on staff at the church, I didn't know any of the elders, and I didn't know anyone at the search firm. Strange as it may seem, I've never actually had a résumé. Bottom line: I wasn't looking. Second, my wife, Lisa, and I had just begun living out one of our dreams. After years of dreaming and scheming, we had recently purchased an old homestead ranch from a ninety-eight-year-old farmer. We bought it with two other families and wanted to raise our kids together on the land. One of the families consisted of my sister and brother-in-law and their four kids, and the other family was one of my dearest friends and his wife and their four kids. Between the three couples, we have eleven children ranging from ages seven to fourteen.

It was all just beginning to take shape. We were raising cattle and tending chickens and planting huge gardens that were yielding hearty harvests. We were repairing the old farmer's fifty-year-old fences so the horses and cattle had safe pasture. My brother-in-law, known as Uncle David to my kids, was building a hog business. By day he was a high school principal, but by night he was delivering litters of piglets that he would feed and fatten for slaughter, hogs that would end up feeding and fattening people all over Colorado Springs. My kids were spending late nights with him in the barn, catching and cleaning newborn piglets, and gaining confidence as amateur veterinarians.

The kids had started their first business: selling eggs to the neighbors. They were learning life lessons and acquiring skills and growing handy with tools. They were driving tractors and trucks and four-wheelers around the ranch. Before the unexpected email dropped in my in-box, we were loving life with the neighbors we had chosen! We had just finished our fifteenth year at the church we love. Our roots were growing deeper in Colorado Springs. The Pikes Peak region had insinuated itself into our souls.

But now it was on. Our roots *seemed* to be loosening.

The unexpected email turned into phone calls, and the phone calls turned into Zoom interviews with the search firm. They had me writing papers and gathering transcripts and report cards from my seminary days. They started running background checks to see if I had a criminal record. They even ran a credit report on us to see if we had any outstanding debts that might be a problem in the future. I underwent a psychiatric exam to see if I was stable, and I sat before a board of theologians to see if I was theologically orthodox. By this time, they knew more about me than my own mother.

After all those boxes were checked, it was time for them to put us in direct contact with the church. They had Lisa and me record a video, introducing ourselves to the elders. In that video, Lisa even shared that she grew up in a suburb neighboring their church. This would be a return home for her. We all started to think, *Maybe this isn't random! Maybe God is in this.* The elders watched the video, and that night the point person with the search firm called and told me, "Something happened in the room when they watched it. You wouldn't have believed it!" They were moved and requested an initial video interview with me.

And, oh, my stars, that first call! I don't know how it could have gone better. There was tenderness, openheartedness, even a hope for the future of that ailing church. Tears were shed. Laughter was shared. The very next day I received a call that they wanted to fly me out there for a face-to-face conversation. From that point on, it just kept snowballing. Over the course of the next three months, they flew me to their church three times.

I have spent my whole life reading Jesus's Great Commission: "Go into all the world and preach the gospel to all creation" (Mark 16:15). I have carried with me from my childhood a God-given desire to change the world. And so, as this process unfolded, occasionally the thought came to me, *Maybe this is how I'll do it. Maybe this is how I'll do more for the kingdom.* (But hold on to that thought for a minute. I'll circle back to it.)

By this time, we had invited our children into the conversation. We knew this would be the biggest decision of their lives, so we listened to them. We sought their input. We heard their fears and protestations. We cried with them. We gave space for their grieving at the thought of leaving. And we prayed with them. But as we prayed, we watched a willingness blossom in all three of them. Yes, they were willing and, at times, even *excited* by the challenge that seemed to be cracking open before the five of us. As a family, we had given our yes to the Lord and our yes to one another.

Then the elders called and said they were flying to Colorado Springs. We were entering the final stages. They wanted to see *our lives* in *our place.* They wanted to visit us at *our church.* And so they did. They attended our weekend services to hear me preach. They spent three hours with Brady Boyd, my boss and pastor, and interviewed him about me. We shared meals together. They met my children. It was a magical weekend, and it felt like the six-month process was coming in for a smooth landing.

The final night of their weekend visit, they took Lisa and me out to a meal at one of the nicest restaurants in town. One of the elders quieted the table and waited for everyone's attention. He told us what he thought about us, thanked us for a great weekend, and acknowledged the grueling process we'd submitted to over the last six months. And then he raised his glass and proposed a toast. Lisa and I both thought, *Oh, man, so this is really happening.* "To the future!" he said. "To the future!" we all responded. And we all smiled, clinking our glasses together in the middle of the table.

As the night went on, they asked us what neighborhoods we were considering. They asked us what schools and soccer clubs we were thinking about for our children. And then they told us that a letter of intent would likely be forthcoming the next week. At the end of the night, we all hugged and told one another how much we had enjoyed these few days together. It was the perfect way to end a perfect weekend. They flew home the next day.

And then, a week later, one of the elders called me. But the call wasn't to talk through a letter of intent. It was to tell me that they were moving on. She said they were sorry to inform me that after six months, they were starting their search over completely. I was in shock. I went numb. I didn't even know what to say. And I didn't know blood could flush out of your face that fast. I remember my cheeks burning like they do after an intense workout. Not because I was mad. I don't even know *what* I was feeling at that moment, frankly. So I sat there quietly—for thirteen minutes—while she told me how much she appreciated me and how great of a pastor she and the rest of the elders thought me to be. It all rang so hollow in that moment. She then started praying for me. I didn't want to be prayed for, but I couldn't cut off someone from praying. So I sat there with the speakerphone on and my head in my hands. And then she said goodbye.

The call was over, and with it six months of my life and the most emotionally charged process I'd ever led my family through. What we thought was going to be a smooth landing ended up crashing and burning right in front of us.

For several months we grieved. It felt like we had been in a wreck and were now suffering from emotional whiplash. But we weren't so much grieving *not* being able to go; for as I said, our friends at New Life Church and the people we were living with on the land were tangled up in our hearts. We were grieving the disruption of soul, grieving what felt like the unnecessary loosening of our roots. And I was grieving the thought that maybe, just maybe, my life might not have as much of an impact by staying put. Remember that whole Great Commission thing? *Will I be able to do as much for the kingdom if I'm not going? And if not, will I ever really be fulfilled?* In short: *Will I be stuck by staying?*

But that was then. Now the dust has settled. As we have healed and our souls have been restored, we are thinking more clearly. We learned so much through the process, too much to summarize here. But here are some of the most important things we learned: God doesn't judge the effectiveness of our lives using the metrics of the market economy, and God doesn't assess the fruitfulness of our lives based on the *quantity* of people we are around but by the *quality* of our service to the people around us.

> Sometimes the most significant thing you can do is *stay* in a place.

And we learned you don't always have to *leave* to build

a life of significance. In fact, sometimes the most significant thing you can do is *stay* in a place—*stay* for the long haul, *stay* and give your life away for the good of *these people* in *this place*.

I Know I'm Not the Only One . . .

As a pastor, I spend my days talking with people. And here's what I know: I'm not the only one wrestling with questions of fulfillment and fruitfulness. I'm not the only one wrestling with feeling stuck.

I'm thinking of millennials who have moved back into their parents' homes, forced there by economics and a faltering job market in spite of their best efforts to gain independence. I'm thinking of parents who never expected to feel held back from their own aspirations by their responsibilities as a parent, who wrestle with feelings of guilt and shame for even having those thoughts. I'm thinking of children who didn't expect to be the sole caregivers for their aging parents. I'm thinking of middle-aged professionals laid off at the apex of their careers because their company knew they could hire someone half their age for half their wage. I'm thinking of entrepreneurs whose businesses crumbled to pieces in a pandemic after years of blood and sweat and scary debt. I'm thinking of hourly workers who can't claw their way to economic stability. I'm thinking of anyone who wrestles with how mundane their life seems when all their friends' social media highlights pulse with adrenaline. And finally, I'm thinking of people who have achieved their goals and dreams and climbed to the top of the mountain they had been hoping to summit, only to find they're just as dissatisfied as before.

In short, I'm thinking of you! Yes, *you*, the one holding this book. And I'm thinking of me. Yes, *me*, the one writing it. It's okay. We don't have to glance away embarrassed. It's okay for us to name the realities we face. We all wrestle with feeling unfulfilled, with feeling *stuck*. We all battle boredom and, at times, suffer from an impoverished imagination that keeps us from seeing the latent potential of the place we inhabit. We all have complex—and sometimes even downright difficult—relationships that, at best, make staying feel like too much work and, at worst, feel impossible, even dangerous. And we all have seasons where we are struck with a sense of failure, and that feeling often colors our associations with the place where we live.

Very often we think the cure for these bouts of self-doubt and unfulfillment and complex relationships will be found in a new life in a new place. And sometimes it will. There are times when a move is necessary; if you have to protect your children from a dangerous and violent ex-spouse, if you need to find healing from a toxic church or work environment, or if you require affordable housing in a different region of the country. If that's you, please protect yourself and your people. Create the space necessary to heal and to feel secure. And do it without any sense of shame.

But there are many other scenarios that will not require a move. And, in fact, there are times when moving only exacerbates the problem. Instead of doing the hard work that is required, the hard work that could lead to personal growth, we bounce, carrying our baggage with us. Maybe we do this because we think the change will change the feelings we're struggling with. Maybe it will. But what if it doesn't?

Having named some of the *internal* forces that keep us moving, I ought to name some of the *external* forces. The cultural moment we inhabit is exerting intense pressure on us, pressure that makes it hard to put down roots.

#Wanderlust

What I am concerned about is an emerging spirit of the age, the American zeitgeist that can be summed up in the hashtag #wanderlust.

We have discovered that, unlike for previous generations, it is quite possible for many of us to see the world. We are no longer restrained to one place as our grandparents were. Marketing strategists, seeing the opportunity, have trained us in the language of the transcendent. Our athletes have become Promethean figures, endlessly powerful, the stuff of legend. They jet to their homes all over the world, and tabloids hire photographers to keep them in front of us. We plaster their faces on downtown skyscrapers while the bright lights shimmer. At least until free agency comes around, and they leave town for the next higher-paying contract. The new sign of success is when we no longer need anyone. We can pay our bills. We have reasonable health. We have risen above it all.

The other side of the fence presents grass that seems greener, at least to the untrained eye and the undisciplined soul. Entire cottage industries exist to instill appetites within us that lead to instability. Marketers are paid good money to make us unhappy with our homeplace and our homely lives. Think about New York City's nickname, the Big Apple. It has been used for decades in ad campaigns by the New York tourist authority. I have friends who live in that stunning city and family members who live around the edges of it, and I myself have made some incredible memories there. I have nothing but love for the big city. And still, the not-so-subtle implication in calling it the Big Apple is that everywhere else is *small*.

Think about the allure and mystique of Paris. The good vibes emanating from Portland. The music scene in Austin. The Rocky Mountain high that can be bought and burned in Boulder. We are schooled in the global magnificence of Dubai, the inimitable significance of Los Angeles, the new money to be made if we can just break into the old money networks in Boston.

For many, there's a gravitational force tugging us toward dramatic landscapes. We descend into the West Rim of the Grand Canyon and suddenly find ourselves. We backpack through Yellowstone and then hitchhike to the Grand Tetons and finally discover how we were made to live. We find a cheap flight to Reykjavik, Iceland, and somehow instinctively know that after four incredible nights of glamping, this landscape has always been in our blood. With our technology, we are only now discovering that the wonders of the ancient world are unnecessarily limited to seven. Throw open the doors. There is no limit to the grandeur.

In short, we live in the age of #wanderlust. We think a move will be the cure for our boring lives.

But what if there are necessary and voluntary limits we must submit ourselves to in order to experience *home*? The climb to find home in the modern world is entirely uphill.

Sending the Demoniac Back Home

The impulse to bounce around isn't anything new. Jesus confronted it when he saw it.

In his brilliant book *The Wisdom of Stability*, Jonathan Wilson-Hartgrove points out that "just as Jesus' movement is picking up momentum, he tells a man *not* to follow him."[1] This is indeed strange coming from Jesus, the man who made a habit out of disrupting people's lives. "Come and follow me" sounded forth from the Savior at least twenty times in the Gospels. Peter and Andrew, James and John, Bartholomew and Matthew, Mary and Martha followed him wherever he went. The list goes on and on. Jesus demanded total allegiance. But in Luke 8:26–39, we meet a man known as the Gerasene demoniac.

Before Jesus showed up, the man was traumatized and troubled, and everyone in the region knew of his sad and complicated life.

> As [Jesus] stepped out on land, a man of the city who had demons met him. For a long time he had worn no clothes, and he *did not live in a house* but in the tombs. . . . (For many times [the unclean spirit] had seized him; he was

kept under guard and bound with chains and shackles, but he would break the bonds and *be driven by the demon into the wilds*.) (vv. 27, 29 NRSV, emphasis added)

The poor demoniac had no family relationships that we are aware of from the text. He was homeless and heartbroken, and everywhere he went, hearts were broken and troubled by his brokenness.

But then Jesus walked ashore and did what Jesus does, healing and delivering and bringing the man back to his senses. Still, Jesus eventually had to leave, for there were other people farther afield who were troubled by the same spirits. They needed Jesus to come their way too. So as Jesus was boarding the boat to cross back to the other side of the Sea of Galilee, the now free demoniac raced down to the shore to jump aboard. He was going to leave his old life of embarrassment and shame, of fractured relationships and frail economy, to run around the region with Jesus! But Jesus said no. Here's how Luke put it:

The man from whom the demons had gone begged that he might be with him; but Jesus sent him away, saying, *"Return to your home*, and declare how much God has done for you." (vv. 38–39 NRSV, emphasis added)

The demons that were driven out of the man were forces that drove him to abandon the place of his flourishing and live among the tombs. He was "driven by the demon into the wilds" (v. 29 NRSV). He had no stability, no friends, no place, even though there was a home right in front of him.

This story suggests to us that the result of the demonic is instability.

And when the demons were driven out of him and into the pigs, the swine ran off. Look at this interesting play in the text: the previously pastured pigs, the pigs that had a home, were now homeless, living among the tombs, cast into the chaos of the deep. Before, it was the demoniac who was on the run; now it was the pigs, while the homeless demoniac was settled and re-homed. This was the first time the man was able to sit still, to stay put.

> Then people came out to see what had happened, and when they came to Jesus, they found the man from whom the demons had gone *sitting at the feet of Jesus*, clothed and in his right mind. (v. 35 NRSV, emphasis added)

The first sign of his freedom was his *stability in place*. This is the first time in the text that the demoniac isn't frantically on the move. So when Jesus had to go and the demoniac tried to follow him, Jesus turned him back, saying, "*Return to your home*, and declare how much God has done for you" (v. 39 NRSV, emphasis added). Return to your home. That's the place for you.

In this story, Jesus seemed to understand stability as *the opposite* of being trapped, the opposite of being stuck!

Trying to live and die in one place over a long period of time is painful. Often the greatest pain inflicted on us comes from those closest to us. Jesus knows this, for his own family "went to take charge of him, for they said, 'He is out of his mind'" (Mark 3:21). Jesus later said, "A prophet is not without honor except in his own town, among his relatives and in his own home" (Mark 6:4).

And like Jesus, we know the difficulty of staying in our homes and in our home country. We want to run, to flee, to go with Jesus to any place other than the place of our old associations, our stagnating pain, our peculiar relationships with our particular family and friends. We think it will be simpler on the other side of the lake. But Jesus won't let us run away.

Jesus, in essence, said to the demoniac: "This is the ground from which you came, and this is the field you were made to work."

This story is the story of a man who finally found enough freedom to quit running. He was so free that he could now *stay*. "So he went away, proclaiming throughout the city how much Jesus had done for him" (Luke 8:39 NRSV).

A Statement and a Promise to the Reader

Now, let me be very clear: I am not writing to romanticize stability in place. Not everyone *can* stay in the same place forever. Not everyone *should* stay in the same place forever. Indeed, I hope by now we have established there are certain times when a move is necessary. There will be those—like Mother Sarah and Father Abraham in Genesis 12—who hear the clear call of God that leads them to a new land. If that is you, let the Lord lead you into your promised land. When a move has become obvious, seek the counsel of your closest companions on the details of what your move should look like. Then go for it! Trust God. Take the leap.

But even Sarah and Abraham ended up settling in Canaan. And most missionaries who feel the tug to go to a distant land are wise to adopt a version of the vow of stability in the foreign land that has now become their home.

Let me make a *promise* to all of you. By the time you're done reading this book, you can expect to learn about the ancient vow of stability that saints all over the world have taken. You will discover the data that social scientists have compiled to detail the costs of our present-day hypermobility. You will realize the benefits—the social, emotional, and physical benefits—of being rooted in place. You will see how your unique skills can contribute to the peace and prosperity of your place. You will be introduced to several compelling figures who have much to teach about honoring your place in this world. You will see how the practices of stability can strengthen your homes, your families, your friendships, your churches, and your communities.

And, finally, even if you are not living in your final destination, this book will help you learn how to be where you are with the very best of who you are. So let's get started!

CHAPTER 2

THE VOW OF STABILITY

Why We Don't Need a New Place to Have a Rich Life

With Christ's help, keep this
little rule for beginners.
—*Saint Benedict of Nursia*

The monk makes these promises in the presence of
all . . . : stability, conversion of life, and obedience.
—*Saint Benedict of Nursia*

SAINT BENEDICT OF NURSIA WAS AN ITALIAN MONK who lived fifteen hundred years ago, and you and I need to know about him.

He was a man familiar with God's love of place. But he also knew the deleterious effects of hypermobility, having observed it in his own day. He had seen the infection spread through so many of the monks. He wrote about a group of monastic contemporaries called the gyrovagues[1] (the Latin prefix *gyro-* means "circle," and the root word, *vagus*, means "wandering"). They were men wandering in circles, they were gyrating spiritual vagabonds, they were moving targets never able to be pinned down. They were like druggies looking for their next hit of spiritual ecstasy. They were homeless, monastery-less, professional conference attendees, Christian couch surfers bouncing from place to place. In a word, they were *rootless*, and we all know that where there are no roots, there is no fruit. According to Gerald Schlabach, after watching this kind of life for years, Benedict described the result: "Always on the move, they never settle down, and are slaves to their own wills and gross appetites."[2]

Writing to his young monkish apprentices, the older Benedict instructed very clearly: "The monk makes these promises in the presence of all . . . : *stability*, conversion of life, and obedience" (emphasis added).[3] We have no problem conceptualizing holy people vowing obedience to the Scriptures, which over the course of decades will result in the conversion of one's life. That is the stock-in-trade of saintliness: obedience that becomes conversion. But Benedict didn't start with obedience and conversion in his monk manifesto. Interestingly, the first vow he called them to make was the vow of *stability*, a commitment to radical rootedness in their particular place; in other words, "Don't leave this monastery. Stay here. You don't need a new place to become a new person in Christ."

But why this vow first? Benedict knew that we don't obey Jesus in general. Obedience is always practiced *in particular*. We practice Jesus's command to turn the other cheek in the presence of annoying family members and demanding neighbors (Matthew 5:39). We practice patience with sleepy toddlers and aging grandparents in an uncle's house around holiday meals that are filled with talk of religion *and* politics (Galatians 5:22). We practice working for "the peace and prosperity" of the particular cities and neighborhoods to which the Lord has sent us (Jeremiah 29:7). The Christian life is practiced in particular places with particular people. Saints are always made *somewhere*.

> The Christian life is practiced in particular places with particular people.

So Benedict thought the first vow should be the vow to *stay*, the vow not to run from the very people and place that God intends to use to make us holy. But staying put is often the hardest thing to do. Sometimes leaving holds the most allure, and old Benedict knew it. He knew that when push comes to shove and life gets hard and relationships grow chaotic and complex, the human instinct is very often *not* to dig in but to *flee*, to start fresh, to burn all the old bridges that keep us connected to a precarious past.

The Cost of Hypermobility

It is important for us to recognize that mobility is not a neutral category. There can be a steep cost associated with our mobility. The American Psychological Association (APA) conducted a decade-long study with 7,108 Americans to see if they could discern if and how moving affects people. Their stated goal was to discover "the relation between the number of childhood moves and well-being."[4] Published in the *Journal of Personality and Social Psychology*, the findings suggest that

> moving is associated with *lower levels of overall well-being*, higher stress levels, and fewer positive social relationships. Frequent moves have a particularly detrimental effect for adolescents, who've been shown to have lower test scores and graduation rates, fewer friends, and higher drug and alcohol use. . . . We know that children who move frequently are more likely to perform poorly in school and have more behavioral problems.[5] (emphasis added)

Now, let me say this: I know scores of people who have moved around the country to follow a parent on active duty in the military. They were in multiple schools in multiple states and still maintained straight As, never did drugs, and never drank a sip of alcohol. They had meaningful friendships and were deeply satisfied with their lives. Their parents created a safe place in the home, and that safe place traveled with them wherever they went. So mobility isn't *automatically* a liability. If that is the life you are choosing or having to live right now, take a deep breath. I'm not trying to come at you with an accusation.

I am, however, trying to host an honest conversation. And the data shows that mobility *can be* costly. The APA researchers discovered that "frequent relocations in childhood are related to poorer well-being *in adulthood*," because the participants in the study were found to have "fewer quality social relationships as adults" (emphasis added).[6] For many young children, the geographical interruption of a move led to the dissolution of friendships.

One more thing to consider: our patterns of mobility often take us away from the larger family superstructure of aunts and uncles who care for us, a cantankerous grandpa who shows his love by teaching us how to fix the small engine on our go-kart, a grandmother who takes us out to her backyard garden to pick berries that'll become the jam for our morning breakfasts, cousins who pace the sidelines at our soccer games and cheer us on. We lose what scholars and psychologists call "social capital"—the riches that come from living in a web of trusting, duty-bound, and obligatory relationships. "The geographic mobility required by many career paths divides families, which provides opportunities for corporations to sell services families used to provide freely—childcare, end-of-life care, emotional and mental support, recreation."[7]

Yes, cheering us on and checking on us, that's what family does when family is working as it should. The elderly making an investment in and helping care for the grandchildren, and the elderly being cared for by their children when they're no longer able to care for themselves. Everyone working together for the continued strength of the whole. But when a relational superstructure like this can be accessed only once or twice a year, around the holidays, something has been left on the table. Remember, mobility is not a neutral category.

With our regular mobility comes the loss of social capital.

The Barriers to Stability

So if mobility can be costly, it's worth asking, What are the barriers to our stability?

Shigehiro Oishi, a social scientist at the University of Virginia, recently published his years-long research on the psychology of residential mobility. He observed,

> Recent research has shown that residential mobility (number of moves for an individual or percentage having moved recently for a neighborhood) is associated with the primacy of the *personal* over the *collective* self.[8] (emphasis added)

Part of the reason we move so often, he noted, is because we have bought into the narrative of the progress of the freestanding person. But Oishi goes on:

[Residential mobility] is also associated with *"duty-free"* friendships and group memberships rather than *obligatory* friendships and group memberships. Overall, residential mobility is associated with lower levels of well-being at the individual level of analysis. Finally, residential mobility is associated with *personal forms of subjective well-being* (based on self-esteem, the verification of the personal self) *as opposed to interpersonal forms* of subjective well-being (based on social support, the verification of the collective selves).[9] (emphasis added)

We move, Oishi concluded, because we have not allowed ourselves to be bound to any *place*, to any *one*, to any particular *community*. We move because we have not committed to a people in a particular place that is worth dying for and dying within. We live outside of and unencumbered from the web of life that could bind us together if we would just stay put.

We have prized duty-free friendships and memberships over *obligatory* ones simply because they are cheaper and require less of us. When relationships are inevitably strained, we find no need to do the hard and often soul-wrenching work to repair them, because we will surely be gone in a couple of years. The duty-free friendships and memberships that we *bounce into* and then *away from* are less valuable— not *ontologically* less valuable, not *intrinsically* less valuable, but less valuable because of what we have *prioritized*: the ascendancy of the free-floating self.

But our forebears thought about things differently. Most

of them had to prioritize "obligatory friendships and memberships" because, well, it was a matter of life and death. There were no other options. You *had* to cooperate. You *had* to barter goods and services. One resident of the community could supply beef to a neighbor who had wheat in abundance. Shake hands and the deal was done. One family would come over and help another harvest their fields, knowing that next month the favor would be returned. The necessary exchange. The reciprocity of relationship. The back-and-forth of life.

These people believed that one was rich, that one was living the abundant life, if they were surrounded by and living within the strength of a larger group of family, friends, and a faith community that was committed—as the ancient Israelites were committed—to leaving the edges of their field unharvested so that everyone could have enough to eat. They believed in the simple joys of bread broken around the table after a long day's work. They were thrifty, and very little was wasted. Even if they lived around a larger and more populous town, they were protected because they grouped in smaller communities. People felt the proper human obligation to one another. People were duty bound to one another and would have felt communal dishonor if they stood idly by and refused to contribute their fair share in the face of the needs of others.

Most communities around the globe today still *have to* live embedded within these obligatory friendships and memberships. Relational webs—not a personal financial safety net—are the only thing to catch them when they fall. Individualism is simply not an option.

For the first time in human history, large swaths of the populace can live under the illusion of autonomy. From the beginning of time, there have always been the privileged few. The Neros of the world, locked away in palaces, playing their violins while Rome burned. Not worrying about anyone beyond their immediate circle. But in our day, the privileged few have turned into the privileged *many*. And with that spike has come a new cultural invention: the single-family home.

Now, of course, the advent of the single-family home is not intrinsically *bad*. And there's a reason that certain people have endless jokes about life with the in-laws. Some families see one another only a few times a year around the holidays, and those days are filled with complexity and anxiety. They are happy to go back to their single-family homes at the end of the week. Fair enough. There's no shame in that.

But we do have to acknowledge that on the timeline of human history, our living arrangements are *new*. And with this newness, we have to ask what we have lost—if we have lost anything at all—when we did away with the old arrangement of multigenerational living spaces. We now live in a societal structure, even when we *aren't* moving, that can increase social isolation. There are fewer people to have to learn to get along with because, to put it simply, there are fewer people actually around us. And so we have come to value the *personal self* over the *collective self*. Our society has jettisoned *obligatory* friendships and memberships for *duty-free* ones. Should we be surprised then that much of our society fails to work toward collective shalom?

It's worth stopping and asking the question: How's that autonomy working out for us?

The Benefits of Being Rooted

In the beginning, God planted Adam and Eve in a garden place called Eden. We will see in the next chapter that *place* is God's first gift to us. But at this point we should ask, Is there an actual *purpose* to place? I think there is. Of the many things that could be said here, I will make three observations.

First, when things are working rightly, place provides *security.* When Abraham Maslow drew up his triangular chart of the human hierarchy of needs in 1943, he was restating what philosophers and anthropologists and theologians had been saying for thousands of years: a place to call home is foundational in the great quest of becoming. Or we could say it this way: place is to a person what womb is to a child. When someone grows up in a safe place, where love is expressed and basic needs like water, food, clothing, and shelter are met, they are planted in the fertile soil in which the body can spring up and the psyche can flourish.

Thinking back to my childhood home, I can almost feel the carpet underneath my feet. The view from my bedroom window down South Eighty-Fifth East Avenue is still fresh in my mind. At night I would lie in my bed while one of my parents knelt down next to me to read me the Scriptures. They would lay hands on my head and pray a benediction as I drifted off to sleep. The layout of the kitchen is easily recalled over thirty years later, and the pantry seemed always to have something in it. The first project I remember doing with my dad was setting a basketball hoop in concrete in the driveway. I remember planting small trees in the front yard and playing baseball in the backyard. My mom played an all-star third base and my six-foot-six dad towered over me from the pitcher's mound. My three sisters were in the outfield, and I stood at home plate with my ball cap on backward, for a time transfigured into a young Caucasian version of Ken Griffey Jr.

Those memories are the fruitful soil of my physiological and psychological development, the incalculable gift of safety in *place*. And all this helps explain the crushing heartbreak of urban homelessness, the grief of refugees spread across the globe and obligated to live in tent encampments, the ache of economic migration that separates workers from their families, and the forced expulsion of indigenous tribes. Place has been pilfered. Home has been lost.

Should there be any question why Jesus, when proclaiming the good news to a weary world, said: "In my Father's house are many rooms" (John 14:2 ESV)? He was, in effect, saying that he had come to redress the ruinous expulsion that sin wreaks all around us. He wanted us to know that in the end, there would be no more refugee camps or homeless veterans in the streets or children sleeping in cars at night. The mission of Jesus was to enwomb the world, to re-home humanity and indeed all creation. And how would he do it? By becoming homeless himself, by divesting himself of his heavenly place, by tabernacling (John 1:14) in a human body so that through his humble life, his gruesome death, his victorious resurrection, and his royal ascension, the human being that lives by faith in him could be guaranteed a home with the Father. Which is the ultimate return to security of place.

Second, when things are working rightly, place nourishes *identity*. We humans are made of physical matter, but the physical matter in which we are raised—the *place* we grow up—ends up *making us*. No person develops in a vacuum. To a great extent, we are all products of our places. Think about Steve Jobs growing up in the fertile Silicon Valley. Think about Bill Gates growing up in tech-savvy Seattle. Think about brothers Steph and Seth Curry growing up with their dad, Dell, who played in the NBA for sixteen years. That life was all they knew. Think about Peyton and Eli Manning growing up with their dad, Archie, who played in the NFL for thirteen years. Think about the youngest Nobel Prize laureate, Malala Yousafzai, growing up in a Pakistan that has long stood against women's rights. It was an upbringing that would only deepen her resolve to fight for the freedom and educational future of little girls. Nurture backs nature into the corner, if only for a minute. Place is one of the primary realities of our development. It becomes a sort of incubator of awareness. Anglican bishop John Inge, himself a lifelong student of place, wrote that place is "the geography of our imagination."[10]

Daniel Kemp Wilson, my maternal grandfather and the man after whom I, Daniel Wilson Grothe, am named, lived almost all of his eighty-six years in northern Idaho. He was the proud son of George Burl Wilson, a farmer and cattleman with a strong chin and a considerably barreled chest.

Together they worked several hundred acres, raising crops and cattle and pork and poultry that helped feed the county. Though I grew up in Tulsa, Oklahoma, I spent my summers in Idaho, working the land with my grandpa Dan. By then he was operating his own forty-acre sod farm. The grass was pristine. There wasn't a dead spot on the property. Grandpa would drive the tractor that pulled a sod cutter, and my dad and I would be on the back, catching and stacking the long strips of sod onto wooden pallets. Then we would get the forklift, grab the heavy sod-stacked pallets, and lift them onto a long flatbed truck.

We would deliver fresh grass for new homes and commercial construction sites all over Washington, Oregon, Montana, and Idaho. It probably won't be a surprise, then, when I tell you that my favorite scent in all of the world is freshly cut grass. And though I spend my days working as a pastor, there is a very particular reason why my wife and I are raising our children on land with all kinds of animals and a large garden: place helped nurture my identity. When God set Eve and Adam down in Eden, he in essence said, *Here is your garden. These are the walls within which you'll be moved to wonder.* We are made of matter, but matter also *makes us.* Place nourishes identity.

Third, when things are working rightly, place affords us the opportunity to *exercise skilled mastery.* The garden place was a gratuitous gift to the first family. It was a place without lack. The generosity of the gift-giving God was on display from the beginning. But on the relatively short list of things that God did *not* give them, we should also mention this: they were *not* given a perpetual utopian vacation. Or to say it positively,

God loved them so much that he gave them meaningful work to do. He gave them jobs, a holy vocation. The human creature is crucial in the ongoing coherence of creation.

A lot of people wrongly assume that work was the result of the fall (Genesis 3). The thinking goes: Adam and Eve sinned, so God punished them and made them get to work. But that won't hold up to the scrutiny of Scripture. Before the fall, we are told that

> God *blessed* them and said to them, "Be fruitful and increase in number; fill the earth and *subdue* it. *Rule* over the fish in the sea and the birds in the sky and over every living creature that moves on the ground." (Genesis 1:28, emphasis added)

> The LORD God took the man and put him in the garden of Eden *to work it and keep it.* (Genesis 2:15 ESV, emphasis added)

Sure, work got harder because of the fall (Genesis 3:16–20). A curse hit the land. "Thorns and thistles" sprang up, and by "the sweat of [Adam's] brow" the chaos would have to be fought against. But we have to keep saying this because the text says it: work is not divine retribution for human rebellion. Work is not God deciding to stick it to humankind. Work is not some post-fall aberration. Work is a blessing (1:28). Work is a gift. And work is intrinsic to the human creature because it is intrinsic to the Creator himself. *God* works, and it follows that because we are made in his image (Genesis 1:26–27), *we* work too.

We see this truth played out every time there is a global recession or a pandemic that leads to widespread joblessness. When the coronavirus (COVID-19) took the world by storm in 2020, many people lost their jobs. Some were furloughed. I had many furloughed friends in the United Kingdom who were still getting paid their normal wage through a government assistance program.[11] But they sat at home for twelve weeks. As I jumped on Zoom calls with them, many were dispirited and despondent. A transatlantic flight away, I was too. One wonders why, being that many had the necessary funds still flowing in to live full lives. The answer lay at the genesis of the scriptural text: the human creature was meant to work, to tend the garden, to contribute to the ongoing movement of the creation story. And when that shuts down and we are no longer able to contribute, something in us shuts down too.

Ellen Davis, a renowned Old Testament scholar, has spent over forty years parsing the Hebrew Scriptures. Much of her focus has been devoted to the creation poem. The command in Genesis 1:28 given to Adam and Eve was a command to steward the earth. It is regularly translated as "subdue," "take dominion," or "rule." Many of us are almost overly familiar with that passage and miss the linguistic force of it. Often the work of a scholar is to make the familiar strange again so that a fresh understanding can arise. And Davis can help us here. She works with the familiar "take dominion" phrase and translates it as "exercise skilled mastery."[12]

God blessed them and said to them, . . . exercise skilled mastery. (Genesis 1:28)

Notice in Genesis 2 that God set Adam in the garden with the responsibility of naming the animals. "Hey, Adam, what do *you* think? What do *you* want to call them?" He didn't give Adam an encyclopedia cataloging the name of each species. He didn't give him a gardening manual. He wanted *Adam* to pay attention to the ordering of the world. He wanted *Adam* to use his imagination. He wanted *Adam* to navigate his way through the earth and develop creational savvy. He wanted *Adam* to get his hands in the dirt. Notice that Adam was practicing husbandry—the proper management and conservation of land and resources—before he was ever a husband to Eve. Husbandry before husbanding. There is something deeply important about that observation. This is the God who not only gives human creatures a place but also gives them permission, the wide lanes of permission to work with and for—but never against—the land.

And caring for that place was the proper exercise of their personhood. Interestingly, the proper English name "Adam" comes from the Hebrew *adamah*, which means "of the ground, land, earth." This creature was the from-the-earth man who would spend his days working the earth, meaning that to work on the land, in a sense, was to work on *himself.* And that is precisely what I feel every time I'm working in our garden. As I'm pulling weeds, I turn to prayer and ask God to weed the anger and darkness and pride out of my soul. Every time I'm building or repairing fences that will pasture our cattle, I ask God to keep me locked up in the safe limitations that will lead to life.

The gift of place is one of the great gifts we've been

given. But it always comes with a purpose: to create security, to develop identity, and to exercise skilled mastery.

The Walls of Wonder

The great British essayist and novelist G. K. Chesterton lived in London in the late 1800s, a time of unprecedented religious insurrection. He stood dumbfounded as people left the faith of their parents and jettisoned the church altogether, denouncing the teaching of the church as too limiting. "Get off our backs! Let us live!" they cried. But Chesterton stood as a prophet among the self-determined exiles and warned them. He knew that to run from the faith of the church was not to be free but to be handed over to a truly tyrannical taskmaster—the self. In his famous book *Orthodoxy*, he wrote about the necessity of staying anchored and the blessing of holy limitations.

> Those countries in Europe which are still influenced by priests, are exactly the countries where there is still singing and dancing and coloured dresses and art in the open-air. *Catholic doctrine and discipline may be walls; but they are the walls of a playground. . . .* We might fancy some children playing on the flat grassy top of some tall island in the sea. *So long as there was a wall round the cliff's edge, they could fling themselves into every frantic game and make the place the noisiest of nurseries.* But the walls were knocked down, leaving the naked peril of the precipice. They did not fall over; but when their

friends returned to them, they were all huddled in terror in the centre of the island; and their song had ceased.[13] (emphasis added)

It is hard to think of a more accurate description of our own day. Our walls have been knocked down, and we have been exposed to the naked peril of the precipice. So many of us live on the move. The geographical boundaries that were meant to keep us safe, to preserve our song, have been disregarded. And for many of us, our souls have been silenced.

We remember that thirteen hundred years before Chesterton came along, Benedict of Nursia was one of the original wall builders. In calling people to live the vow of stability, Benedict drew up a blueprint and began constructing "a wall round the cliff's edge" so we "could fling [ourselves] into every frantic game" and make the world "the noisiest of nurseries." That is what the vow of stability was meant to be, after all—walls that keep us from tumbling over into a life of untethered rootlessness.

"Stay put," Benedict said. But sadly, too many have read this as a *prohibition*—"Thou shalt not leave!"—when they should have read it as a *protection*. The biblical concept of fidelity can thicken our emaciated twenty-first-century notions of freedom. Benedict was not trying to *lock us out* of a great big world that's just waiting to be explored; he was trying to *invite us into* a rich and textured communion with the people and the places we have been given. There is a sort of calculus at play here that only makes sense in the kingdom of God: those who are willing to lose the freedom of a thousand different options will find they have everything they need right in front of them (see Matthew 10:39; Luke 17:33; John 12:25).

> Those who are willing to lose the freedom of a thousand different options will find they have everything they need right in front of them.

There are ultimately two ways we can understand these geographical walls set up by the vow of stability. We can see them as walls of *withholding* or walls of *wonder*. We can see stability in place as an entrapment, an impediment, a prohibition that's keeping us from personal fulfillment. Or we can see it as a protection, an unspeakable blessing, an invitation to deepen our commitment to the people and the place where we have been planted—a deepening of roots that will bear much fruit.

CHAPTER 3

THE GIFT OF PLACE

A New Perspective on Belonging

The LORD God took the man and
put him in the garden of Eden.
—*Genesis 2:15 ESV, emphasis added*

WE HAVE JUST SEEN IN CHAPTER 2 THAT MANY ancient Christians felt a call to take vows of stability in a given place. But it's worth asking *why* they felt that. From where did this conviction come? In this chapter I make the case that their conviction and commitment to stability came from their understanding of who God is and how God works. From the first pages of Scripture, we see that God loves the physical world and the particularity of place. Or here's another way of saying it: God is a materialist.

We know, of course, that God is spirit (John 4:24). But my contention is that God is not spiritual in the way so many of us expect. Actually, many of the first glimpses we get of him are so thoroughly *material*: "Now the LORD God had planted a garden in the east, in Eden" (Genesis 2:8). We are taken into that garden and introduced to the God of the green thumb.

We Christians know Genesis 1:1, that famous poetic flourish that informs us of God's inexhaustible creativity: "In the beginning God." But before we can go forward, we must go backward, back to what things were like before the first day. In the second verse of the Bible, the ancient storyteller flashes back—*way* back—and helps us imagine what was going on *before* the creational beginning. We are told that antecedent to creation there was an amorphous nothingness, an utter formlessness, an abysmal emptiness. The Hebrew phrase for "formless and empty" is *tohu wa-bohu*, a clever linguistic tongue twister that is meant to communicate just how tightly tangled the chaos was (Genesis 1:2).

But out of the long primordial silence and the deep void came an eruption of life, from the darkness an explosion of radiant incandescence. "Let there be light" crackled through the cosmos, and at the sound of God's voice, Brother Sun and Sister Moon danced, forever endowing this world with blazing solar beauties and deep lunar mysteries. It was not good for water to be alone, so the Lord reached into the belly of the abyss—just as he would later reach into the belly of the slumbering Adam (Genesis 2:21–22)—and pulled out the dry land, giving the wild seas the companionship of something to crash into. Land stands up out of the depths as the blessing of demarcation and delineation. The Genesis 1 poem sets us down in a world of physical matter, a world of rocks and trees and skies and seas. There were seeds bursting forth and plants beginning their vertical pilgrimage skyward and reefs teeming with every kind of fish.

Old Testament scholar Ellen Davis points out that the first blessing from God in all of Scripture was given to the *animals*—to the livestock, the fish, and all the winged creatures (Genesis 1:22).[1] Lest we humans think we own the joint, lest we think that "taking dominion" is synonymous with dominating the creatures, God first creates and blesses all the creatures, great and small. Genesis 1 tells us that we humans show up later to the party, a good party that has already been blessed, which means our job is to find our way into the preexistent blessing without messing it up. (We, of course, eventually do mess it up in Genesis 3, but let's not get ahead of ourselves.)

A slow reading of the first chapter of the Bible shows a material world that is bursting with benediction. The poem is written from the perspective of a poet who has a front-row seat to watching God's happiness in real time, watching him enjoy the liveliness of his creation.[2] Can you imagine having a front-row seat in the theater of creation? The writer gives us a sevenfold literary consummation to tell us what it was like: God saw that it was good (Genesis 1:4, 10, 12, 18, 21, 25, 31). God so loved the world, yes, and it didn't take him until John 3:16 to start loving it.

At the apex of the creation poem, we get a slightly unexpected turn, a downward descent into the dirt. God gathers a clump of clay with divine intent and lovingly donates his breath of life. As the lungs fill and the chest cavity expands, consciousness cracks open.

> "Let us make mankind in our image." . . . In the image of God he created them; male and female he created them. (Genesis 1:26–27)

Slow down or you will miss it. In the telling of the old story, the materialist God does not out of nothingness *speak* humanity into existence. No, he is the manual laborer. He uses his hands and *makes* humanity out of the raw muddy materials—the raw *matter*—of his good creation. Eugene H. Peterson put it this way:

The Latin words *humus*, soil/earth, and *homo*, human being, have a common derivation, from which we also get our word "humble." This is the Genesis origin of who we are: dust—dust that the Lord God used to make us a human being. If we cultivate a lively sense of our origin and nurture a sense of continuity with it, who knows, we may also acquire humility.[3]

We rise from the dust, and Father Abraham, the first pilgrim who flung himself out into the mysteries of God, knew it. Locked in intercession for the people of Sodom, Abraham prayed with an awareness of his earthy origins: "I have been so bold as to speak to the Lord, *though I am nothing but dust and ashes*" (Genesis 18:27, emphasis added).

Yes, God is so devout a materialist that he actually *became* material. The apostle John said it this way: "And the Word became *flesh* and dwelt among us" (John 1:14 ESV, emphasis added). In the very womb of the Virgin Mary was woven the God-man. Christ the Lord was nurtured in utero. This is the God who so believes in the created order that he allowed himself to be enwombed in amniotic fluid and connected to his mother by umbilical cord. And everything about his life was earthy. He was circumcised on the eighth day (Luke 2:21). He had family and friends and complex relationships. He regularly went to the temple (Luke 2:41–52). He was baptized in water (Luke 3:21–22). He went to weddings and sometimes even supplied the wine (John 2:1–12). He took a nap in the back of a boat and knew all about thunderstorms (Mark 4:38–40). He was a fisherman and was known to cook a nice meal for his friends over a fire he had built (John 21:1–14).

The woman with the issue of blood didn't hope to catch positive vibes from Jesus; she wanted to touch the hem of his garment (Matthew 9:21). He washed the disciples' calloused feet and dried them with his robe (John 13:1–17). He picked up little children and blessed them, and I'm sure kissed them on the cheek before he turned them loose to their parents (Mark 10:13–16). And on the night he was betrayed, he broke bread and poured the wine of the new covenant (Matthew 26:17–30). Can you see the unflinching *physicality* of life in the kingdom of God? You don't have to have a sixth sense to see that this is the God of the five senses.

In Jesus's incarnation, we see the God of blood and bone, flesh and fragility. His bodily presence in the world was as real, as *material*, as nails driven into a cross outside the city gates of Jerusalem. You can't crucify a spirit; you can do that only to a *body*. And when he was raised, he wasn't some precious eternal soul floating through Galilee. Thomas touched his scars. The bodily resurrection of the Son of God is the statement once and for all that our God is a materialist.

If you don't love the world of the flesh, you're doing it wrong. If you don't sink down into your five senses and notice the gifts all around you, you're missing out. For our God is a materialist.

The First Gift God Gave Humankind

But what does that have to do with anything? Why should God's materiality matter to us? It matters because it shows us in advance what kind of life God gave us and what kind of work God expects of us. So far, we have seen that the creation story is a story of God's gratuitous gift-giving. But notice this crucial detail in the text: the first gift that God gave humankind was the gift of *place*. The writer of Genesis said,

> The LORD God took the man and *put him in the garden of Eden.* (Genesis 2:15 ESV, emphasis added)

We should not be in a hurry at this point in the story. God gave Adam a vibrant place within which his life could unfold to flourishing. It was a garden place with a vibrant ecosystem, a place to belong, an all-encompassing place made up of particular places to find meaning and enjoyment. The creek running through that corner of the garden over there. The grove of olive trees to the south that needed tending if there was to be oil. The vineyard of grapes hanging fat on the vines, waiting to burst into the finest wines. The lush foliage, the natural herbs, the weeds needing to be pulled in the vegetable garden, the insects, the earthworms, and the migratory birds. The meandering brook that sings only by the accompaniment of rocks.

Here, Adam, receive my grace.

Here, Eve, is your place.

But now, for a brief moment, we need to observe and make explicit what God did *not* give the first family. He did *not* give them a transcendental spiritual existence that hovered above the *humus*, the holy ground beneath their

> **The first gift that God gave humankind was the gift *of place*.**

feet. Adam and Eve were *not* simply eternal souls borrowing bodies for a minute until they could get to their real destination someday. Earth was *not* made to be a warm-up act, and humans were *not* set down here to do busywork until God could beam them up to the starship *Enterprise* that's on its way to an immaterial heaven.

We have been looking at the first pages of Scripture, but this would be a good moment to look at the last page to remember where this story is headed.

> I saw the Holy City, the new Jerusalem, *coming down* out of heaven from God, prepared as a bride beautifully dressed for her husband. And I heard a loud voice from the throne saying, "Look! *God's dwelling place is now among the people*, and he will dwell *with them*. They will be his people, and God himself will be with them and be their God. 'He will wipe every tear from their eyes. There will be no more death' or mourning or crying or pain, for the old order of things has passed away." (Revelation 21:2–4, emphasis added)

The consummation of the story shows heaven *coming down*. God's dwelling place is moving into *our space*. He's coming to dwell *with us*, right here, on this dirt. But we Westerners have been shaped by a couple of hundred years of "enlightened" thinking that would lead us to believe that the world and the flesh are of the devil and that only the spirit—the spirit*ual*—is good. This is not a new malady among the human race, for the apostle Paul wrestled with the Gnostics in his own day; they believed that the physical world is intrinsically evil, and that salvation comes through the apprehension of secret spiritual truth. And we are their offspring. But we didn't get this disembodied, anti-creational way of thinking from the God of all flesh or from the Scriptures he intended for our instruction. No, Adam and Eve were embodied beings. They were given a garden to work, *not* a manifesto of doctrinal formulas. And it wasn't just any old garden. They were given *this* garden, called Eden, situated eastward, with a river flowing out of it that became the four great rivers of the region: the Pishon, the Gihon, the Tigris, and the Euphrates (Genesis 2:8, 10–14).

Here, Eve, receive my grace.

Here, Adam, is your place.

The Bible is our book, and as we look at the first page, we see that the first gift God gave humankind was the gift of *place*. And the contention of this book is that his intention has not changed. God wants us to find home. God wants us to experience belonging.

But How Do We Know *Which* Place?

Now comes the next logical question. How do we know *which* is the place God has prepared for us? Is it just where circumstances take us, or do we get a say in it?

I'll start by saying there is no exact formula for discovering where to live. As much as I wish there were, there just isn't one. The Bible is filled with a multiplicity of scriptures and stories that show us a complex range of possibilities. Abraham and Sarah suffered the heartache of leaving their homeland to go find a promised land that God would show them along the way. Hagar understandably ran from her pain but was stopped and turned around by the God who wanted her to find his unexpected goodness, even in a scary place. Joseph was sold by his brothers to slave traders who carried him to Egypt. Joseph's descendants became so mighty in Egypt that they were enslaved as cheap labor before being delivered into the wilderness of bewildering provision. And the ancient people of God endured long stretches of exile in several foreign countries.

Complexity surrounds this topic like walls around an ancient fortified city. But we are not completely locked out. There are some doorways that can lead us to discovery. I believe there is a constellation of considerations that, when paid attention to, will yield some crucial clues in our quest to discover which place it is that we should live, which place it is that God has for us.

So how do we know? Here's a little place-discovery acronym (DROPS) I've created that I think can be helpful and memorable:

Desire
Relationships
Opportunity
Purpose
Skills

First, *desire*. King David, the ancient psalmist of Israel, famously wrote: "Delight yourself in the LORD, and he will give you the desires of your heart" (Psalm 37:4 ESV). Now, I don't think David was propounding some sort of wish-fulfillment theology, where it's God's job to bless us with the sports car we've always wanted. Rather, David wanted us to know that as we keep in step with the Lord, longings are awakened in us and desires arise, desires that are from God's very heart. Your heart will tug you in a direction. There may be a city that is buried deep in your heart. On the other hand, you may know a region of the country in which you absolutely *don't* want to live; you have no *desire* for it. Pay attention to that. It may just be God's way of directing you and making things clear. There may be an insatiable desire to be near immediate family. There may be a desire for a certain kind of landscape. It might be something—an ache, a longing, a tug—the Lord has put inside you. As you work to discern your geographical place in this world, pay attention to those desires. Desire isn't everything, but it's certainly not nothing.

Second, *relationships*. As I reflect back over my life, I have found that in seasons of transition the Lord has almost always led me *through* relationships *to* a place where I *have* relationships. And as I listen to people tell their stories, I find that thread emerges regularly. So pay attention to your desires, and don't be surprised if the Lord wants to position you around at least one or two people you love.

Third, when trying to discover where your place is, watch for *opportunity*. Throughout the Scriptures, God shows himself to be the good provider. Sometimes a geographical move is necessitated when work dries up. Bills need to be paid. Bread needs to be won. And often the best way to tell where to go is to pay attention to the doors of opportunity that open up. It's not a foolproof way of discerning, but do not underestimate the role that an opportunity can play in discovering where God might want you to plant.

The fourth clue is *purpose*. We all are made with a desire to make a contribution to the world. We all possess unique giftings and special graces that flow through us naturally. And without a place to exercise those gifts, we wither. So when you're looking for your place in this world, pay attention to the options that allow you to live with purpose.

Finally, when trying to discern where you belong, pay attention to the kinds of places that need your *skills*. Certain places might need you. Silicon Valley needs software engineers. Nashville needs world-class musicians. The oil fields of Oklahoma need people who know that kind of work.

None of these individual considerations should be treated in isolation; but when considered as a whole, these clues can help you find your place. Because, as we see from the first pages of Scripture, our God has a particular place just for you.

PART II

THE *PRINCIPLES* OF STABILITY IN PLACE

CHAPTER 4

HONORING YOUR LOCATION

The Membership Benefits of Place

I take literally the statement in the Gospel
of John that God loves the world.
—*Wendell Berry*

AT THE BEGINNING OF OUR JOURNEY TOGETHER, you met an old Italian monk named Benedict who called for vows of stability in place. Now it's time to meet an old monkish farmer from Port Royal, Kentucky, who has lived those vows for eighty-six years. His name is Wendell Erdman Berry.

Berry is one of the most sophisticated men of letters of the last hundred years. As a poet, essayist, and novelist, he was awarded in 2010 the National Humanities Medal by President Obama for outstanding achievements in history, literature, education, and cultural policy. But he is a farmer first, and all of his writing has been one long extended parable arising from his family's work in the fields.

The undulating hills that make up his Lane's Landing Farm are the same hills that his Kentucky ancestors have farmed for seven generations. The long line of agrarians from which he comes has kept Henry County in corn, wheat, alfalfa, soybeans, and—before the damning surgeon general's report of 1965—tobacco since the early 1800s.

In his early twenties, Berry left the only life he had ever known in rural Kentucky to attend California's prestigious Stanford University. He was fellowshipped at the university and invited to study under Wallace Stegner, a literary legend and Pulitzer Prize–winning novelist. Almost overnight, Berry had gone from a small farmhand to a high-society sophisticate, from a blue-collar worker to a white-collar conversationalist at the country club. His star was on the rise, and in his midtwenties, Berry found himself gallivanting around the globe as a Guggenheim Fellow, which took him to France and Italy to study with some of the world's greats. From there he moved to the Big Apple to teach at New York University (NYU) in the Bronx.

But when he turned thirty, Berry and his bride, Tanya, suddenly packed their bags and returned home to Kentucky. Why would he do this? Why squander his growing influence and the opportunities the big city could afford? His writer friends and all the university sophisticates gave him their condolences, for they knew this would be the end of his career, the death of his literary dreams. One does not simply walk away from the world's publishing headquarters without paying a steep price. But Berry was willing to lose his career if that's what moving back to Kentucky meant, because in gaining the whole cosmopolitan literary world, he was losing his old ancestral agrarian soul. Berry knew the words of Jesus, who himself had grown up in a small subsistence farming community:

> Very truly I tell you, unless a kernel of wheat falls to the ground and dies, it remains only a single seed. But if it dies, it produces many seeds. (John 12:24)

After years of working in the fields, Berry was comfortable letting his career fall to the ground like a seed and die, trusting that God could raise up a harvest of quiet happiness and good work on the other side of this temporary death. And the harvest has indeed come. In eighty-six years, he has written eighty books without having ever owned a computer! He works in his unadorned study that overlooks the Kentucky River, and he writes with paper and pencil. When he's done, he takes the binder to Tanya, his wife of sixty-three years, who carefully edits it for him before sending the book or essay or poem off to a publisher.

But when he takes that pen and presses it firmly to paper, what has he had to say? What does Berry truly care about? His body of work is too vast to summarize here. I know from the outset that I can only scratch the surface of his contribution. You will have to let this chapter serve as a gate that opens into a much wider field to be explored. For now, though, I will highlight a few of his most significant themes. I am limiting our exploration to three values by which Wendell Berry would have us live.

Value 1: A Love of—and Devotion to—Our Places

In an earlier chapter, we discovered that God is a full-bodied materialist, which is to say that matter—the physical stuff of our very existence—matters to him. Too many Christians are accidental Gnostics. We have been trained to think that physical matter doesn't matter, that all that *truly* matters is the "spiritual" stuff that happens in the invisible realm. We think of ourselves as eternal souls trapped for a time in ephemeral bodies. We think the earth is a ticking time bomb, and that just before it blows, we're going to fly away to our *true* home in the clouds. One of our most popular hymns says it without the slightest hint of blushing: "I'll fly away!"

N. T. Wright, a New Testament theologian, has spent forty years fighting this new Gnosticism. He famously quipped that with the way so many Christians talk about the material world, you would think that John 3:16 actually said, "God so *hated* the world, that he *killed* his only Son."[1] But from Genesis 1 to Revelation 22, the Scriptures give us a different story—a story of a God who, from the beginning, was found "walking in the garden in the cool of the day" (Genesis 3:8), and who, in the end, resurrects a New Jerusalem, the bustling and robust holy city of God that has a river of life cutting through the middle of it while the tree of life bursts with the sweetest-tasting fruit. This holy city plays host to the marriage supper of the Lamb (Revelation 19:6–9), where people from every nation, tribe, and tongue are healed as they feast on the sumptuous delights (Revelation 21–22).

Wendell Berry learned the goodness of creation, learned that the material world matters, by living outside, by giving all his attention to his Father's world.

> I take literally the statement in the Gospel of John that God loves the world. I believe that the world was created and approved by love, that it subsists, coheres, and endures by love, and that, insofar as it is redeemable, it can be redeemed only by love. I believe that divine love, incarnate and indwelling in the world, summons the

world always toward wholeness, which ultimately is reconciliation and atonement with God.[2]

And Berry believes that as we discover just how much God loves the world, we also discover our deep calling and the essence of the human vocation: to love the world just the same, to give it our full attention, to notice its beauty, to be enraptured by its mysteries. The God who loves the world would love for us to rejoice in and be in awe of the purple mountain majesties that can be seen only in the early morning sunrise. The God who loves the world would love for us to notice the beauty of the Canada geese migrating south for the winter in their flying-V configuration—flying in that sacrificial formation where one goose at a time goes first, taking the hit, flying out front, absorbing the brunt of the trade winds, playing the Christ figure, mimicking the Messiah before "dying" and being "buried" in the back of the line until a resurrection of strength comes again. Wendell Berry wants to ask us, Do you really love the world?

But before we move on, Berry would have us be even more specific. We haven't been called to love the world *in general*. No, we have been called to love *in particular* the little worlds that we all inhabit. For the man who loves women *in general* is called a philanderer, an infidel, while the man who loves "the wife of his youth" *in particular* and continues loving her into his old age is called faithful. And the faithful will experience dimensions of blessing that the philandering pleasure seeker will never know, even as the bodies pile up in his endless search for sexual conquest. Elsewhere, Berry wrote, "No matter how much one may love the world *as a whole*, one can live fully in it only by living responsibly *in some small part of it*" (emphasis added).[3] Generalization is the death of intimacy; abstraction the archenemy of love. So it makes sense that God so loved the world that he gave his only begotten Son to Mary and Joseph who lived in the cramped little city of Nazareth in Galilee! Love makes a big difference when it gets small.

To keep his eyes trained and his heart attuned to the beauty of his own place, Berry takes Sabbath walks and writes poetry. In one of his poems, he wrote, "I keep an inventory / Of wonders and uncommercial goods."[4] Wonders and uncommercial goods are all the things that cannot be marketed and sold. Berry seems to know that you cannot drop-ship to your doorstep the simple joys of walking through fallen leaves. And he has learned to notice the fallen leaves as little composting miracles, death decomposing itself through the winter months to be resurrected into new life in the spring. The "wonders and uncommercial goods" all around us cannot be purchased; no, they can only be enjoyed. And the mysteries that we behold *around* us have a way of metabolizing *within* us and manifesting *outside* of us in a kind of reverent holiness. As the poet Mary Oliver observed, "Attention is the beginning of devotion."[5]

For all these years, Wendell Berry has been calling us back to a sort of Genesis 1–2 betrothal to our places. But too many of us have failed to see their beauty. We talk about the little towns that so many people grew up in, and we call them "nowhere," rural haunts, godforsaken places. Berry would have us know that there's no such place as *nowhere*.

And it would be good for us to remember that they said the same kinds of things about Jesus's upbringing: "Nazareth! Can anything good come from there?" (John 1:46). That place, they thought, was too backwoodsy, too provincial.

Jesus coming from Nazareth is a statement once and for all that there is no such place as nowhere. The God of eternity past moved into the "middle of nowhere" so that from then on, every place is a *somewhere*.

In a poem, Berry pierces through our very worst misconceptions of place:

> There are no unsacred places;
> there are only sacred places
> and desecrated places.[6]

No unsacred places. No godforsaken places. No such place as *nowhere*. For God is there with the creatures he has created. And if God is there, that place will forever be a *somewhere*.

But Berry reminds us that there are desecrated places, places that are populated with people who don't seem to know that their job is to love the particular world of rich particularity in which they live. So the question becomes: Will you treat your place *sacredly*? Will you treat it as the holy ground upon which God has visited you?

Jason Peters, an English professor, aspiring hobby

> The God of eternity past moved into the "middle of nowhere" so that from then on, every place is a *somewhere*.

farmer, and lifelong student of Berry, summarized what he learned from Wendell Berry of Lane's Landing: "Not to hope for a better place but to be worthy of the one I'm in."[7]

For God so loved the world. And we should too.

Value 2: Membership in a Thriving Local Community

The ancient Greeks were a philosophical bunch, wrestling with and wondering about the vicissitudes of the human experience and the meaning of life. They understood that life would be shot through with challenge and heartache but also with meaning and joy. They wanted to know: What does the good life consist of? What makes a life truly rich? These are the same questions that arise throughout Berry's six decades of writing, sometimes explicitly but more often implicitly. And Berry has been concerned with these questions for good reason, because he knows we are sick.

His landmark book *The Unsettling of America* was written in 1977, and things have only gotten exponentially worse since then. Some will miss that fact because they have enough money to mask the problem. At least for now. Our deep pockets are buying us time from having to address our near-fatal wound, which is our placelessness, our lack of community membership, the destruction of our small farms and rural communities, our loss of familial ties that comes from our transience, and the collapse of our neighborliness because we're a mass of strangers.

New York Times book reviewer Donald Hall, after reading Wendell Berry's work and getting a glimpse of his life, wrote, "Berry is a prophet of our healing."[8] Which is to say, he has discerned and articulated a way forward that can lead to the abundant life that Christians have always been so concerned with. That is, if we will just listen to him.

So what does Berry have to say about what makes a life truly good? One word: *membership.* Yes, his most oft repeated response to that ache for blessedness, for happiness, for human flourishing and welfare, for a prosperity that goes beyond the power or the impotence of our pocketbooks is a call to *membership within a thriving local community.* But membership, for Berry, is a complex cocktail of concerns. We know that, in an unbalanced ecosystem, when *one thing* is off, the *whole thing* is off. And so it is with a healthy community.

According to Berry, the ecosystem that makes up a healthy community is balanced and life-giving when it is composed of wholesome family relationships and rich friendship, safe housing and a sustainable food supply for everyone, opportunities for deep education and meaningful work for all, culminating with space for weekly Sabbath leisure, routines of worship, and opportunities to serve. When things are working rightly, safety is experienced in the streets because everyone is committed to similar visions of neighborliness that lead to flourishing.

There's bartering between the butcher and the cattleman. The doctor takes care of the electrician's ailments, and the electrician keeps the doctor's office powered up. The craftsmen and the carpenters build the schoolhouses so the teachers and tutors can educate their children. Membership in a community like this ensures the elderly are valued and cared for by the children and the children are instructed and shown the way by the elderly. In a vibrant community, those with specialized needs are not pushed to the edges by the strong; instead, they stand with strength and call for the preservation of innocence and conservation of joy. And it's not just people-to-people relationships that make up a healthy community. A local community thrives when the people properly care for the land and its water and all their creatures. Membership is communion with *God*, with the *ground*, and with *one another* expressed within a local community of people bent on doing good.

Berry's vision of membership is achieved when everyone takes their place and gives their best.

Grandma Weezie of Juliaetta

My grandma Louise "Weezie" Wilson is eighty-nine years old and lives in the northwestern panhandle of Idaho. The town is called Juliaetta ("Julie-etta") with a population of 697. She lives on the land her father bought in 1918 from the Nez Perce tribe.

Grandma Weezie's father, my great-grandfather, was Haralambos Athanasios Asimakoupoulos, a Greek immigrant. Born in Monastiraki, Greece, in the late 1800s, Haralambos was the youngest of ten children. When he was in middle school, his father died and his mother walked him down to the shore of their port on the Aegean Sea. She put him on a boat all by himself and said something like "I love you" and "You'll have a better life in America," though he had never spoken a word of English. It was the last time she would ever see him, and weeks later, he washed ashore at New York City's Ellis Island. The year was 1907.

Because people couldn't pronounce his name, Haralambos shortened his name to Harry and started working the railroads on his way out west. When he got to Idaho, he took the money he had saved and over time bought two thousand acres of farmland along the Clearwater River. The train tracks that Harry worked are between the river's edge and the small house he built for his wife and six children up the Catholic Creek Canyon. My grandma Weezie is one of those children.

Recently I visited with her for four days. We sat in her living room that overlooks the river and talked while we watched a team of bald eagles dart and dive to skewer trout and steelhead with their razor-sharp talons. She told stories that spoke of membership in a thriving community. She told me about walking down to the train tracks with her five-year-old twin sister and a note from their mother pinned to their shirts. The train conductor would see the girls from a distance, slow the train down to a halt, and reach his rugged hand down to lift them aboard. The note gave instructions that the girls needed to go eleven miles to Lewiston to the five-and-dime store to get some groceries and other necessary goods. But let me clarify something: this was *not* a passenger train! It was a train carrying gruff characters and salty machinists and foulmouthed men from around the community who were working for their daily bread. They were hauling goods and materials and felled trees from upriver that would become lumber for houses and a new general store in town. But the train conductor knew these little girls, he knew their parents, and they all shared a common trust, so he took the girls into town and brought them home on his return trip a few hours later. They were *five years old*! I yelled out loud when Grandma Weezie told me the story. She said, "Honey, they don't do that anymore, do they?"

She told me another story of her dad meeting a German immigrant worker on the railroads. His name was Peter Wagner, but for some reason my grandma never knew, they all called him Fritz. This was in the 1930s, a wildly tumultuous time for Peter's people in Germany, and Fritz was alone in the United States. But his homelessness was quickly reversed. Grandma said,

Daddy let him live in the shack out back and Fritz kept it spotless. He became a hired hand around the place. Daddy knew what it was like to be an immigrant all alone in a new world, so he was going to take care of Fritz. He never charged him a dime. Fed him all his meals. Fritz became a part of the family. Chores. Mucking the stalls. Working together to repair the barn. That man worked hard every day of his life, and he died of a heart attack in the pasture behind the barn. We were all there when it happened. I got down on the ground to hold him when he collapsed. His head was in my lap when he passed from this life. I must have been ten or twelve years old. And we buried him in the cemetery in Juliaetta.

Can you imagine? A man all alone in a foreign country, speaking a foreign tongue, with no immediate family, while his homeland was burning down! And then, out of nowhere, he's swept up into a family of eight and a small town that cared for him and held him close as he died. This is what Wendell Berry means when he speaks of membership.

Grandma Weezie told me about scores of transient drifters coming up the canyon from the train tracks to the front door of their house. "Hobos" she called them without the slightest hint of condescension or meanness; it is a time-bound technical term from that era. These vagabonds crisscrossed the country by hopping on and off trains under the cover of darkness, stowing away among the supplies. And they just kept coming to the front door, knocking and presenting themselves in their utter desperation. "Momma always had them do a chore—maybe chop some wood or feed the animals—while she fixed them a hot meal. But she fed every one of them."

One day another knock came. Weezie's mom asked the man at the door, "How did you know to come up here?" He said, "Another guy living under the bridge posted a sign: 'There's a friendly family up the canyon.'"

My grandma Weezie grew up in a world where everyone seemed to be aware of their interdependencies. Everyone knew they had to work together. Of the town's one-room schoolhouse, she said, "All the teachers were just like aunts and uncles." Even if these people didn't know about the apostle Paul, they knew he was right, they knew they were "individually members one of another," sharers in a rich and inescapably intertwined destiny (Romans 12:5 ESV). They lived out Wendell Berry's dream, the dream he's been writing about and calling us into all his life: the dream of deep membership in a thriving community, a community that takes responsibility for one another.

In his novel *The Wild Birds*, Berry puts these words on the lips of Burley Coulter:

> The way we are, we are members of each other. All of us. Everything. The difference ain't in who is a member and who is not, but in who knows it and who don't.[9]

In our cultural moment of cheap and duty-free friendships, we are in need of growing up. And we will grow up as our roots grow down, down, down into the soil of our local places. For significant pockets of our planet play witness to the fact that you can have a place in which to sleep at night but still be *homeless*. You can be around a bunch of people without ever being *peopled*. But it doesn't have to be this way. Membership is available to all of us, if we'll just give ourselves over to it.

> We will grow up as our roots grow down, down, down into the soil of our local places.

Value 3: The Joy of Hard Work

The final value we will briefly discuss in this chapter, and will develop a bit more in a later chapter, is a value you might expect to find in a farmer like Wendell Berry: the value of hard work. But Berry takes it a step further and calls us to discover the *joy* of hard work.

We have tried to escape the sweat and sorrow promised in Genesis—only to find that, in order to do so, we must forswear love and excellence, health and joy.[10]

God is first introduced to us as a gardener, and Adam and Eve were made to be the superintendents of that garden. They were made *from* the dust (Genesis 2) and were daily *covered in it*, which means that to try to run from the dust of the earth is really to run from *ourselves*, from our very identity.

Berry also reminds us that we were made to use our *bodies*, of the inherent *physicality* of our connection with and contribution to the world. To our grandparents, that would seem so obvious as not even needing to be said. But if you are one of the many adults sitting at a desk for fifty hours a week or a child growing up today, this could be an important reminder. The World Health Organization (WHO) says we are experiencing a "global epidemic" of childhood inactivity.[11] Kids used to play without having to be told to do so, but now, in this digital age of screen oversaturation, four out of five children from the ages of eleven to seventeen aren't getting the physical activity they need, and their cognitive development and social skills are suffering for it.

Charting a Path Forward

My wife and I have been reading and learning from Wendell Berry for many years now. And as a result, we have made changes to our lives. I mentioned earlier that we live on a ranch we bought with my sister and brother-in-law and one other family of dear friends. We subdivided it into three parcels, but we all share the whole of it. We are three families with eleven kids between us. But why are we living on this land? We are *not* living on this land as some sort of attempt to nostalgically retrieve an old vision of America. And we are certainly *not* living on this land as a way of escaping the city. Our kids all play club sports in town, and I drive them to school each day on my way to work. We are very much involved in the life of our community.

We organized our lives this way, first, because we wanted to practice a purposeful membership. On the ranch there are six adults helping to speak into the development of eleven children. Of course, each parent is the primary source of instruction for their children, but the other adults all play an active role in encouraging and teaching and developing all the children living on the land. Each adult possesses unique perspectives and skills that enrich everyone. As each adult lives a wholesome life in front of and around the children, their social capital grows, and layers of security and trust are deepened. And the kids have friends everywhere they look.

And the second reason we organized our lives this way? We are trying to build a strong work ethic and an understanding of how life works into our children. On the ranch, we currently have 6 horses, 9 beef cattle, 10 goats, 40 pigs, 150 chickens, 6 ducks, 11 dogs, and what feels like a thousand feral cats that roam the fields and live not by bread alone but by every vole and field mouse that proceeds from the ground below. Many of these animals are breeding and delivering litters of offspring. In fact, as I'm writing this chapter, my sister Christine is texting me pictures of a mama sow that has delivered eight piglets within the last hour, with more on the way. The children are all helping to catch the piglets, clearing their airways and cleaning them up. And you should see their smiles!

My kids have known about God's good design for life all their lives. They also know the reality of death as they've had to bury animals they've raised. Lisa and I have established a sort of working ranch ordinance with our children that you have to earn your shower, earn your dinner, and earn your sleep every night. Another way of saying it might be: Come in dirty, come in hungry, and come in tired. Use your bodies and use your imaginations. Play. Climb trees. Chase the animals. Splash in the creek. Tend and treasure and do your best to notice the gifts of God's good creation all around you.

The kids help us build fences so we can rotate the animals into fresh pastures. They help us round up and weigh the cattle. They help us castrate the little piglets. They help us build chicken coops and collect eggs and hay the fields at the end of summer so we will have plenty of hay for the winter months. I'm sure we're not doing it all right as parents, and I know we have plenty of room for growth. But I do know that our kids are learning a love for their place, they're learning to use their bodies, they're learning about and falling in love with the God who first appeared to us as a gardener, a manual laborer (Genesis 1). We have Wendell Berry and my maternal grandparents to thank for a lot of that.

Some of you may be thinking, *I could never do that. I'm not a rancher! And I'd never have the time.* For starters, I'm not a rancher either. I'm a pastor and my wife is a real estate broker. We have very full lives that keep us going. So do the other families living on the ranch. But you'd be surprised at what three families with similar commitments can do *together* when they live with Berry's concept of membership in mind.

Most of the people holding this book in their hands do not live on land like this. Many of you live in neighborhoods or apartment complexes or dorm rooms, and you have limitations in what you can do. Even so, Wendell Berry has some recommendations for you. He would say, have some life around you that needs to be tended every single day, such as plants that need to be watered or a small vine of tomatoes on your apartment balcony that needs to be cared for. Maybe you have a little backyard and can raise some hens that you can nurture that, in time, will nurture you with fresh eggs for your morning breakfast. Maybe your neighborhood could use some fresh flowers every spring in the common areas. Maybe you can rally the neighborhood elders and the young children to help you keep it up. Maybe you can plant some trees that you yourself will never find shade under but that others will enjoy into the future.

Even at eighty-six years old and with a significant reduction in strength, Wendell Berry still finds these daily routines to be reasons to get out of bed in the morning. "Dutiful work" he calls it. As you lovingly get your fingers down into the soil of your place, the place will begin to sprout vines that climb up into your heart.

I think it is only fitting that one of America's chief public intellectuals is a farmer, as were so many of the ancient prophets of Israel. So listen to the old farmer in Kentucky.

Fall in love with and be devoted to your place, put in the effort to create a meaningful membership with people in your local community, and work hard with your hands to make the place better. And remember, "The difference ain't in who is a member and who is not, but in who knows it and who don't."

CHAPTER 5

HONORING YOUR RELATIONSHIPS

People Are the Great Purifiers

Wounds from a friend can be trusted.
—*Proverbs 27:6*

Love difficult people. You are one of them.
—*Bob Goff*

MAYBE ONE OF THE LEAST GLAMOROUS THINGS you can do with your life is to stay in the same place with the same group of people—friends, a spouse, a handful of extended family, a local church community—for a really long time until you die. And while it is unglamorous, it may well be the most powerful thing you can do.

Mother Teresa is known to have quipped, "If you want to change the world, go home and love your family." And she categorically refused to accept people into the work of the Missionaries of Charity in India who were looking to leave a robust relational network back home. Of course, there were Catholic nuns and monks who were following the call of God to seek entrance into this new vocation. But Mother Teresa could spot a spiritual thrill-seeker a mile away, someone who would turn serving the poor into self-gratifying voyeurism. She also could easily identify someone who was *running away from* a community in search of a more enlightened one. She knew if she accepted them on those terms, they would find a reason to run away from *her* community too.

Thomas Merton also knew the difficulty of staying with a group of people over the long haul. Merton moved into a monastery in rural Kentucky in 1941, then a twenty-six-year-old man, while the ink on his priestly papers was still drying. But things became exponentially more difficult when, within the next decade, he had become an international figurehead.

He was the Michael Jordan of contemplative spirituality. He was a brilliant thinker whose literary works had found their way into the hands of presidents and popes. Even the Dalai Lama built a trip to the United States around a visit to see Merton at the monastery in rural Kentucky. And this was no ordinary monastery either. This was the Abbey of Our Lady of Gethsemani, the longest-running monastery in the United States. Merton was the leading figure in the leading monastery in a country that prided itself on leading the world.

Now Merton, a famous Trappist monk, felt trapped, closed tight within the confines of these church walls with people who seemed so dull, so ordinary, so average. Most of the brothers didn't have the soaring intellect he had. Most of the brothers hadn't been exposed to and would never be conversant with the work of the continental philosophers as he had and was. These brothers were possessed of a simplicity of spirit that the apostle Paul commended to us. There were so many times over the twenty-seven years Merton lived in Gethsemani Abbey that he ached to live in the middle of the big city, to be wined and dined by the big publishing houses, and to live with constant access to the power structures. He could barely stand it. He wanted to run.

And Merton would have been the perfect candidate to run. He was born in France in 1915, but his family fled to New York to escape the madness of World War I. His mother, Ruth, was from Queens. So they moved there, into a small place with her parents. But almost overnight Ruth became ill. Stomach cancer was eating her alive, and before long she entered her rest. The now-heartbroken Merton was only six. His dad, Owen, grieved his way around the globe, with Merton bouncing around behind him. The boy was living in the wobble and wake of his bereaved father. They moved from Manhattan to Cape Cod, then back to New York before heading to Bermuda. After a year there, eight-year-old Merton was sent back to New York by his father to live with his grandparents. After a failed relationship, Owen left Bermuda and came to New York to retrieve him. They moved back to France, and then over to England, before ending up in Rome.

It is not lost on me that the world's leading contemplative voice had moved at a dizzying pace. Maybe he became a contemplative, taking the vow of stability—the vow to live with the same people in a particular place *until he died*—because stability was all he ever wanted but could not have. Maybe that is why, despite his desire to run from Gethsemani, he stayed another twenty-seven years. Until he died. He was only fifty-three. It's not insignificant that the monastery in which he lived was called Gethsemani. That is the place Jesus considered *running from*, the place from which he cried out for deliverance, the garden where he groaned in deep intercession to see if the cup of death could be avoided. He prayed, *If it be thy will, let this cup pass from me. Is there any other way, Father?*

Indeed, Gethsemani was the place and his brothers were the people who would help purify Merton into a man of God for the world. Toward the end of his life, Merton reflected on just how important it is *to stay*. He wrote,

> By making a vow of stability the monk renounces the vain hope of wandering off to find a "perfect monastery." This

People are the great purifiers. implies a deep act of faith: the recognition that it does not much matter where we are or whom we live with. . . . Stability becomes difficult for a man whose monastic ideal contains some note, some element of the extraordinary. All monasteries are more or less ordinary. . . . Its ordinariness is one of its greatest blessings.[1]

In his own Gethsemani, Thomas Merton learned that people are the great purifiers.

Why We Run

But we don't always stay around long enough to let that purification take place. Often we run, and one consequence of our running is the loss of what we left behind—namely, our friends or the people who could have become our friends. And many of us find ourselves lonely because of it.

Now, let me say that some people are lonely not by any fault of their own but because the circumstances of life have been cruel. They find themselves shut in senior care facilities while a global pandemic has locked their family and friends out. Because a topsy-turvy economy shifted, leaving them furloughed or jobless, others are driven back home to their parents and away from the life and the friends they had made. Relational momentum is interrupted. The people who find themselves in these positions have my deep compassion.

Yet others are lonely because they are *flighty*. They are the unwitting or the unwilling. They either *don't know* where to stay or they *won't* stay in any place long enough to let roots take. They follow the route of Owen Merton, bouncing about instead of following Thomas Merton's example and rooting down.

Why do we run? Sometimes it is *our pathological avoidance of conflict* that keeps us on the move. There's no point in ignoring the truth: if you're going to have friends, at some point the honeymoon phase will be over and you'll find yourself frustrated or annoyed or jealous or suspicious. Your friends will have differing political views that will rub you the wrong way in four-year cycles. Your friends will have the means to take better vacations, and that could stir resentment if you're not careful. Your friends will discipline their children differently and allow them to do things you would never let your kids get away with. Your friends will say things—sometimes wittingly, sometimes unwittingly—that give you the opportunity to take offense. Here's the cumulative effect of all this: you will have ample opportunity to break from your friends over the years.

In the moment of offense, it may feel easier to cut ties and leave. We don't want to do the hard work of facing one another, working through the difficulty, naming the hardship, confronting the things that have led to the breakdown. So we go quiet. We stop calling. We try to avoid them by walking down a different hall at the office. We change churches. We unfriend them on social media. We bolt, but we never go empty-handed. We always end up carrying offenses with us wherever we go.

If we are going to have friends over the long haul, we are going to have to overcome the quick fix of conflict avoidance when the annoyances arise. Because that shortcut always leads to a relational dead end. The ancient vow of stability can help us here. While most of us don't live in a monastery, the monks have much to teach us. One monastery in the midwestern United States has this as a part of their vows for anyone seeking entrance:

> We vow to remain all our life with our local commu-
> nity. We live together, pray together, work together, relax
> together. We give up the temptation to move from place
> to place in search of an ideal situation. Ultimately there
> is no escape from oneself, and the idea that things would
> be better someplace else is usually an illusion. *And when
> interpersonal conflicts arise, we have a great incentive to
> work things out and restore peace.* This means learning
> the practices of love: acknowledging one's own offensive
> behavior, giving up one's preferences, and forgiving.[2]
> (emphasis added)

So you may be wondering, what do I do when I come to a relational impasse? A wiser, older pastor friend, Garvin McCarrell, has told me for decades that "the shortest distance between two people is the truth." Get together and talk; but before you talk, *pray.* Ask the Holy Spirit to purify your motives. Ask the Holy Spirit to keep you from saying anything that will further the damage. Ask the Holy Spirit to enable you to cooperate with his restorative work. Then when you get together, name your frustrations. Be specific. Say, "This is how it made me feel when you said . . ." Ask questions, such as "Is my read of the situation in line with how you see it?" "Is there anything I'm doing that is frustrating you?" or "How can I be a better friend to you?" And if you have anything to repent of and apologize for, do that without equivocation.

A friendship that isn't able to shift into this confrontational space with grace is a friendship still in its infancy. For as old King Solomon said, "Wounds from a friend can be trusted, but an enemy multiplies kisses" (Proverb 27:6).

How the Fruit of the Spirit Grows

As a young child, I grew up with parents who helped me memorize and fall in love with the Scriptures. One of the iconic passages from the apostle Paul burrowed deep into my soul. It is found at the end of his letter to the Galatian church, and it's known as the section on the fruit of the Spirit. We had a song about it, and my three sisters and I sang it often in our house, usually because one of us was being impatient or unkind and we needed patience to show and kindness to grow. It was a joyful tune, sure to shoot a smile across a previously furrowed brow.

But let me say this: there is nothing precious about how the fruit of the Spirit is grown in us. And I'll say this too: the fruit of the Spirit is not grown in abstraction. The fruit of the Spirit grows from the limbs of our lives as we slowly become trees planted by streams of living water (Psalm 1:3). It is the wind of unkind words that beats against us in yearly cycles that, after it has passed, strengthens the young sapling. In the spring of the year, we produce the fruit of kindness.

The dry spells of despair move in, and yet somehow we bud and blossom with fragrant joy. Again, I say the fruit of the Spirit is not grown in us by precious abstractions. It does not magically appear. No, we burst forth with *patience* after suffering long stretches with insufferable people. We are *good* on the other side of people treating us badly, we extend *love* to people who are mean, we demonstrate *self-control* as people come at us and vent their anger.

When the conditions around us are unfavorable, our first instinct is to uproot and shift over to new soil. Maybe the grass *is* greener, we think, and the fields yield finer harvests elsewhere. But as we stay, and as we truly learn to pray, the muck of someone else's immaturity slowly composts and ends up fertilizing faithfulness within us. And, over time, the fruit of the Spirit bursts forth from our lives. What is fruit for? Fruit is to be eaten. It is for our nourishment. On a sweltering summer day, it hits our taste buds with flavor that makes the heart glad and the stomach satisfied.

People are the great purifiers. We grow in holiness as we honor our relationships. Just as Thomas Merton did in the Gethsemani monastery. And if we are willing to submit to the slow growth of the fruit of the Spirit, we, along with the world around us, will be able to "taste and see that the LORD is good" (Psalm 34:8).

CHAPTER 6

HONORING YOUR SERVICE

What Your Skills Can Do

Life's most persistent and urgent question
is, "What are you doing for others?"
—*Martin Luther King Jr.*

A COUPLE OF YEARS AGO I WALKED INTO A COFFEE shop on a slow Friday morning and picked up a mocha and a copy of the *Washington Post*. With computer screens becoming so prevalent, I like to have a paper in my hands as often as I can. There was a story that day about the Queen of Soul, Miss Aretha Franklin, who had just entered her rest with family and friends at her side in her Detroit home. What a woman and what a gift. She was an artist deserving of our endless #respect. Then I hopped over to the sports page to see that Max Scherzer had another dazzling performance on the mound for the Washington Nationals. It's no wonder he's won three Cy Young awards already!

But then I stumbled onto an article that journalists Mary Jordan and Kevin Sullivan had written about President Jimmy Carter and First Lady Rosalynn Carter.[1] The story stopped me in my tracks. Carter was the thirty-ninth president of the United States, and he was in the Oval Office from 1977 to 1981. He had a relatively short political career before becoming president. He served as a Georgia state senator from 1963 to 1967 and as the governor of the Peach State from 1971 to 1975. But then, as a dark-horse Democratic candidate, and after being tied for twelfth place in the early presidential polling, he rose unexpectedly to fill the highest office in the land.

Who *was* this man from the South moving all the

way up north to the White House to lead the nation? The answer: a second-generation small-town peanut farmer. It was only in 1954—just *twenty-three years* before he became president—that a devastating drought hit his hometown of Plains, Georgia. The net profits for the Carter family farm that year were $187.[2] The local economy in Plains is still flagging all these years later. In the national census taken in 2000, the median household income was $26,719, and nearly half of the eight hundred residents lived well below the poverty line.

Maybe that's why the *Washington Post* article startled me. It said that Jimmy and Rosalynn Carter still live in Plains. When they closed up shop on their stint in Washington, DC, they could have moved anywhere in the world. They could have called in political favors and joined the governing boards of multinational organizations and made good money on the speaking circuit while living in a gated community in the suburbs of some large city. It's what presidents do these days. That seems to be the template.

But that's not what the Carters did. They moved back into their small home in their small town and have spent the last forty years serving people that folks in the big cities may see as small. Because of this, I have come to think of them as the President and the First Lady of Place. Regardless of our political persuasions, we can all learn so much from Jimmy and Rosalynn Carter. I'll name three lessons from these icons of stability, which can, in turn, help us honor the people in the places we have been called to serve.

Value 1: The Lesson of Living Faithfully

Eugene H. Peterson understood discipleship to be "a long obedience in the same direction."[3] One who is following Jesus, he thought, will be found faithful for the long haul, will be tracking on dependable and trustworthy trajectories. The faithless are flighty, bouncing here and there and everywhere, but the faithful live as fixtures. The lives of Jimmy and Rosalynn Carter bear witness to such a truth. At the time of this writing, they have been married for more than seventy-four years! And the way they met couldn't have been scripted by even the most imaginative novelist.

> Carter can recall the day his wife Rosalynn was born: he was three and lived next door to her family. His mother, a registered nurse, helped deliver Rosalynn (born Eleanor Rosalynn Smith), and brought her son over the following day to meet his new neighbor. Little did either one of them know, they would end up having one of the sweetest love stories of all time.[4]

When asked what their marriage means to him, Carter said, "The best thing I ever did was marrying Rosa. That's the pinnacle of my life."[5] He lived through the economic undulations of the Great Depression and was plunged into the unpredictability of life on a navy submarine; he navigated a nation through the frigid uncertainties of the Cold War and the perilous heat of the Iran hostage situation; he negotiated an unprecedented peace between Egypt and

Israel and won the Nobel Peace Prize in 2002. But even as so much was changing around him, he always went home to Rosalynn.

Financial Faithfulness

We've already seen that because of devastating droughts in 1954, the Carter family farm had net profits of $187. But after President Carter finished his four-year term, in 1982, more bad news was waiting for him back home.

Written into the law of the land is a clause that distances presidents from the daily details of their businesses. The founders didn't want conflicts of interest driving presidential policies. So Jimmy Carter put his business in a blind trust, and he didn't speak with his trustee for four years. When he started in the White House, the company was thriving. When he packed up the Oval Office four years later and returned home, he discovered a business on the brink of going belly-up. They had more than one million dollars' worth of debt, and creditors were calling because they knew they were dealing with someone of great influence.

Along the way, some friends and advisers suggested declaring bankruptcy. But Carter would have none of it. His parents had taught him that if you give your word, you follow through. You may have decent money, they said, but if someone can't trust that you'll do what you say, you don't really have much at all.

So Jimmy, fifty-six at the time, came home from Washington, DC, and went to work as the executor of the family business. He started planning the way forward. He called his creditors and told them he'd make it right somehow.

He started crunching numbers and totaling up the value of assets, like the large peanut warehouse they owned in town. He was able to work a deal to sell the business that ensured all his creditors would get paid. He didn't walk away with any money, but the dependability of his word was intact, which is worth far more than a quick infusion of cash.

Church Faithfulness

Jimmy Carter grew up with parents who took him and his siblings to church. "We are the Carters. We go to church," he said.[6] And through all of these years, and even after holding one of the most powerful offices in all of the world, Jimmy and Rosalynn have never stopped going to church. Every Sunday you'll find them at Maranatha Baptist Church in Plains. But they don't just *attend*, they *contribute*. I'm not primarily talking about contributing money, though, of course, they do that too. I'm talking about the contributions they're making in the lives of these saints.

Since moving out of the Oval Office and back into this small, rural community, Carter has taught over eight hundred Sunday school classes! He pores over the Scriptures through the week and shows up on Sundays to teach young and old through the Sermon on the Mount or the Ten Commandments or the poetry and pathos of the Psalms. The Carters *could* spend their weekends on a private island somewhere owned by some influential billionaire, but they get up, get dressed, and get to the house of God to gather with their friends and neighbors. They pray for people, they listen to their stories, they know their names, and they gently leverage their influence if and when there are needs they can help meet. People travel from around the world to attend his Sunday school class, but it's the local people at Maranatha Baptist Church in Plains who have gotten the very best of the Carters' saintly stability after all these years.

Value 2: The Lesson of Living Simply

Another thing a thoughtful observer might notice about Jimmy and Rosalynn Carter is that they have lived simply.

After leaving the White House, every president is expected to open an office, a center through which their advocacy work goes forward. Jimmy Carter was no exception, and in 1982 he opened the Carter Center in Atlanta. He chose Atlanta because it is 158 miles due north of Plains, and he knew it would be more accessible for visitors and other elected officials. Work could get done more efficiently there. So Jimmy and Rosalynn drive up to Atlanta one week out of every month to have a full slate of meetings. A journalist was touring the office with them when she discovered they've been sleeping on a pullout couch in the office for decades. Are you kidding? From the White House to a pullout couch? It seems so surprising for a past president, but it becomes unsurprising the more you pay attention to the simplicity of their lives.

Carter flies commercially while other former presidents fly privately. He's done his own remodels on the simple house they've lived in for decades. He's even knocked out walls and opened up new rooms! Rosalynn says it's work he's learned to do after years of helping build houses for Habitat for Humanity.

He is, after all, a child of the Great Depression. He comes from a generation that had to develop the skills to make do, a penchant for thrift and frugality. When the *Washington Post* journalists were following him around Plains to write their story, Jimmy and Rosalynn made their regular evening walk to a friend's house for dinner. They ate off paper plates and drank water out of plastic red Solo cups. Then they walked the half mile back home. This is a man who could demand that a presidential motorcade escort him wherever he wants to go. Instead, he slowly and methodically walks around his childhood hometown, greeting everyone he sees. He is, by a landslide, the cheapest president in modern history for the Secret Service to take care of, and that is primarily because he lives so simply.

One of the things that drives Americans to move is our constant quest for more—*more* money, *more* square footage in a home, *more* influence, *more* opportunity, *more* allure that calls to us from distant places. But the Carters are a testimony to the fact that rich joy is often found in frugality, that less can be more, that fulfillment rises from rootedness. And the irony should not be lost on us: our constant quest for *more* frequently leads to *less* fulfillment.

> Our constant quest for *more* frequently leads to *less* fulfillment.

The beautiful treasure that comes to people who have lived well over the long years is the gradual awareness of what really matters. In their old age, the Carters know what King Solomon learned later in life; namely, that it's "better [to have] a little with righteousness than much gain with injustice" (Proverbs 16:8). The Carters have experienced and lived out what Paul told his young protégé Timothy: "Godliness with contentment is great gain" (1 Timothy 6:6). The Carters have discovered that what Paul told the Romans is true: "For the kingdom of God is not a matter of eating and drinking." It's not a matter of filling yourself up with all the delicacies of this life and gorging yourself on all the opportunities you can find. No, the kingdom of God is about living simply and steadily into "righteousness, peace and joy in the Holy Spirit" (Romans 14:17). And they have embodied that in the simple confines of Plains, Georgia.

Value 3: The Lesson of Living as a Servant

Finally, the Carters have lived as servants.

Sadly, servanthood and modesty are not often associated with the presidency. But Jimmy Carter is different. This is the man who confounded everyone who worked with him when he insisted on carrying his own luggage onto *Air Force One*. This is the same man who broke presidential protocol when he wouldn't allow the military band to play "Hail to the Chief" at important government functions with other heads of state. As Sullivan and Jordan pointed out: "Carter doesn't even have federal retirement health benefits because he worked for the government for four years—less than the five years needed to qualify."[7] Humility. Modesty. Simplicity. Frugality.

These virtues were developed in him from an early age. After graduating high school in 1941, Carter was accepted into the US Naval Academy in Annapolis, Maryland. He graduated in 1946, just after the end of World War II when things were settling down in our nation. He and Rosalynn were married in 1946 and spent the next few years building a family. But in the early 1950s, Carter headed out to sea.

He was working on a submarine, extremely dangerous work in those formative years, and while on a stopover in Bermuda, Lieutenant Carter and his shipmates were joined by some British officers. A party was to be thrown, for life at sea was hard. But the British officials made it clear that it was a party for whites only. Young Lieutenant Carter was incensed. He had grown up in the hotbed of racism, but his Christian faith thrust him into a life of firm resistance against the scourge of ethnic hatred. He canvassed the ship, and using his influence and the strength of his quiet but forceful persuasion, he made it clear that such behavior was not acceptable—if they all couldn't go to the party, then none of them would go. In the end, the entire crew refused to attend, showing an interracial solidarity that much of America was not yet ready to embrace.

Even as a young man, Carter showed he would serve his black brothers, no matter if it cost him his career.[8] This wasn't Carter's first encounter with the evils of racism, and it surely wouldn't be his last.

In 1953 Carter's father, Earl, became gravely ill, and the peanut farm was on the brink of failure. His mother, Lillian, was suffocating under the stress of the looming loss of her husband and the near bankruptcy of the family business. Having read the words of Jesus all his life, Carter was poised to practice them in a costly way. He was ready to lay down his promising military career and go back home. It was the right thing to do, he thought. He would obey the fifth commandment and honor his father and mother. He would deny himself, take up his cross, and follow Jesus back to Plains. It wasn't long after Carter returned home that his father and hero died. It was as if Earl Carter finally felt safe enough to die, knowing that someone was there to take care of Lillian and sort out the farm.

But another fight was looming. Schools were ordered by the US Supreme Court to desegregate. Rosa Parks was standing up for blacks in the South by staying seated in the front of a bus in Montgomery, Alabama. And Carter's commitment to his black brothers and sisters was being tested afresh. Robert Strong summarized the moment:

> An organization called the White Citizens Council was formed to maintain the segregated status quo in the South, and its membership blossomed across the region— including Plains, Georgia. Carter was heavily pressured to join the organization in 1958 and was the only white male in Plains to refuse. The council's members boycotted Carter's business, but he stubbornly held out.[9]

Jimmy Carter was *the only white male* in town to refuse! And the city council boycotted his already struggling business. The financial screws were being tightened on the Carters because of his radical insistence on racial equality. He had read his Bible. He knew from the very first page of the Scriptures that all of mankind was made in the image of God (Genesis 1:26–28). He knew that God was the God of every tribe, tongue, nation, and people group (Revelation 5:9).

And though Carter was threatened with becoming "less" in his own community because of the stand he was taking, his influence was steadily growing. For as we see with Jesus, growth in the life of the Spirit comes in direct proportion to our willingness to become less, our willingness to *die* to self. The road to greatness is the road paved with self-sacrifice.

Jimmy Carter became greater on the other side of his suffering. He could be trusted with caring for a nation because he had spent decades caring for the most overlooked people in our nation. In 2002, at the age of seventy-eight, he was awarded the Nobel Peace Prize "for his decades of untiring effort to find peaceful solutions to international conflicts, to advance democracy and human rights, and to promote economic and social development."[10]

Serving People into New Homes

The Carters have long enjoyed a simple life of stability in Plains. They've been there for ninety-six and ninety-three years, respectively. But they know the gift of stability in place cannot be received without a safe place to lay their head at night. From a very early age, Carter seemed to know this. As a thirteen-year-old, he started buying houses! A presidential historian wrote,

> By the time he was ten, the boy stacked produce from the family farm onto a wagon, hauled it into town, and sold it. He saved his money, and by the age of thirteen, he bought five houses around Plains that the Great Depression had

put on the market at rock-bottom prices. These homes were rented to families in the area.[11]

Carter understood that families would need safe housing with a reasonable rent to be able to survive the Great Depression. So he—a *teenager*—provided it for them.

When he left Washington, DC, decades later, that understanding would only be amplified. For four years he lived in the White House, the most iconic house in the nation, but when he got back to Plains, he moved back into his old house.

Carter is the only president in the modern era to return full-time to the house he lived in before he entered politics—a two-bedroom rancher assessed at $167,000, less than the value of the armored Secret Service vehicles parked outside.[12]

But Carter knew he had work to do, because the poverty rate in Plains was at 40 percent. Almost one-half of the town was scraping by, and they were trapped living in an insecure housing situation. So he got to work, teaming up and building homes with Habitat for Humanity. He leveraged his strength and influence in building over forty-three hundred houses! He hasn't just *lived* stability in place; he has spent his life helping people *find* stability in place. People who were once unstable because of homelessness have now become rooted in their new homes.

Jimmy and Rosalynn Carter have not spent their lives asking, "What can these people and this place do for us?"

Instead, they have lived asking, "What can we do for these people and this place?"

It sounds like they've been listening to the Jesus they've been preaching about all these years in Sunday school, the Jesus who said,

> Do you want to stand out? Then step down. Be a servant.
> If you puff yourself up, you'll get the wind knocked out of
> you. But if you're content to simply be yourself, your life
> will count for plenty. (Matthew 23:11–12 THE MESSAGE)

The Vocational Intersection

So how do we discover where our skills can come together to help cure the ills of the world?

Frederick Buechner, one of the spiritual masters of the last century, wrote, "The place God calls you to is the place where your deep gladness and the world's deep hunger meet."[13] He says that your deep gladness and the world's deep hunger are a sort of intersection. The things you care about, the things you have spent a lot of time on, and the things you do well because you have spent a lot of time on them are precisely the things you can do to satisfy the world's deep hunger. Or I could say it this way: you don't have to become someone else to do something significant. Your life and your skills and your passions can coalesce, can "gather to a greatness" in the place that you come from for the good of the people around you.[14]

It makes me think of the tax accountant in our church

who has loved accounting since his teenage years. Because of his expertise, he was promoted to vice president of one of the nation's largest accounting firms. And every year, he helps widows and single moms and struggling families navigate the uncertain terrain of their year-end taxes. For free. He doesn't see it as charity. He isn't looking for acclaim. He loves doing it because it is the place where his deep gladness intersects with the world's deep hunger. People need their taxes done, and he knows how to do them.

You don't have to become someone else to do something significant.

It makes me think of an older couple in our church who absolutely love caring for babies and toddlers. Over the years, they have taken into their home more than one hundred foster children, nurturing them, praying for them, tucking them into a warm bed at night, and giving them the gift of stability. They have found where their deep gladness intersects with the world's deep hunger.

Jimmy and Rosalynn Carter didn't have to find new skills and a new place to make their mark on their world. And you don't have to either. Let your deep gladness and the world's deep hunger become an intersection, the location in which you carry out your holy vocation.

CHAPTER 7

HONORING YOUR PRESENCE

Everywhere You Are Is Sacred

Spend the afternoon. You can't take it with you.
—Annie Dillard, *emphasis added*

FOR NEARLY EIGHT DECADES, THIS "CHRIST-haunted"[1] planet has been stalked by a woman born in Pittsburgh, Pennsylvania. The year was 1945. The baby girl was born Meta Ann Doak. The world knows her today as Annie Dillard.

Young Annie was raised in an affluent family. She was raised to be a lover of theater and an appreciator of fine music. Her father, Frank, was enamored of Dixieland jazz and was known to dance a jig. Her mother, Pam, was hilarious and was a dancer too. So the Doak household seemed destined to give the world a little girl whose mind pulsed and paced and danced like notes up and down a musical staff. With her curiosity and inquisitiveness, Annie played the role of bookworm, digging her way through and burrowing into the classics and into a deep and subterranean understanding of the way a good story is told. She descended into the depths of drama, learned the texture of tragedy, climbed the literary heights of victory. Sometimes it takes good fiction to tell us the truth, and in those classic novels, Annie discovered the way the world works.

We sing that dark Advent carol "What Child Is This?" in twelve-month cycles, and, of course, we sing it about the Christ child born in Bethlehem. But it's apparent that the people in young Annie's early orbit were asking a similar question: What kind of child *is* this?

Her years under the care of her parents were spent playing

outdoors. One winter morning she flung herself downhill on a sled, careening out of control, until she crashed and smashed her nose to pieces. The very next day there was fresh powder, so she went back out—because she must not have broken her nose the right way the first time—and broke her nose again! She spent summers at her grandparents' place on the shores of Lake Erie, splashing and skiing and fishing and burying her little body in the sand. She played softball expertly and only gave up playing at age fifty-five! She foraged through the forest and watched the fall foliage catch fire. Her husband, Bob, wrote, "She was an avid collector of both rocks and insects. She had a chemistry set and a microscope with which she found a single-celled world full of wonders."[2] And that childhood love of and exposure to nature resulted in a lifetime of literary achievement.

Annie Dillard is recognized as a renowned wordsmith, a virtuoso, a voice unlike any other in modern American letters. From the Pulitzer Prize to the Guggenheim Foundation Grant Prize and all the way down the list, she has won all the honors a writer can aspire to. Paul Roberts of the *Toronto Globe and Mail* reviewed one of her books, saying that it "places Dillard more firmly than ever among the very greatest of American writers."[3] But how was her writing born? Can we trace the genesis of her genius? I think we can.

Henry "the Bore" Beston

All of her life, Annie was a voracious reader. Her library cracks with crooked stacks of books and looks like what you would expect from a storied savant. The dog-eared pages and the scribbled margins are marks of her decades-long mastery. As a young woman, she picked up a book from the acclaimed naturalist Henry Beston. She had high hopes for this book, hopes that soon toppled to the ground face-first like a little Pittsburgh girl on a sled. It took only a few dozen pages into the book for her to know this wasn't where she should look for an imaginative read of the world she had grown to love. Diana Saverin told the story:

> One of the books she read that fall was *The Northern Farm*, a 1949 memoir by Henry Beston that chronicles an agricultural season in Maine. It didn't prove to be a satisfying read, but it did change her life. In one of her journals—filled with a mix of musings, observations, notes, and doodles—Dillard began an entry with the title, "Why I didn't like this book." She wrote, "It was a bore. Not only did nothing happen, okay, but there was no trace of mind. As a naturalist he didn't teach me a *thing*. He didn't even bother to look up fireflies. As an observer of the social scene, which is a boring thing to be in the 1st place, he's ordinary and conservative. No imagination."
>
> As Dillard kept writing, though, she realized something: what Beston lacked—knowledge of the two enzymes that allow fireflies to make their light, imagination, and a "trace of mind"—she could provide. And in that moment of *I could do better*, the idea for *Pilgrim [at Tinker Creek]* was born.[4]

A horrendously disappointing book changed Annie Dillard's life. This was the spark that set fire to the literary phenom we now know. She couldn't just put down the book and leave it alone. Instead, she filled pages of her journal with her ire. The book, for Dillard, didn't *feel* right. It didn't stir the deepest longings. There was nothing in it that made the heart race or the soul ache. There was no tragedy or triumph. There was nothing that made you want to *dance*. It turns out that the jazz she grew up listening to had trained her emotions to need *more*.

If she had stood face-to-face with Henry "the Bore" Beston, she might have said something like, "You aren't feeling it right." Because *feeling* is what Annie Dillard is known for. Ask any of her readers. And if you read Dillard and walk away unmoved, the onus is on *you* to prove to the rest of us that you're still alive. One *New York Times* book reviewer wrote, "There are passages in all Dillard's work, in fact, when her response to what she sees and feels and hears is so intense as to make one believe she is speaking in tongues."[5]

Here's one of the initial lessons we learn from Dillard's process of discovering what she was made to do: sometimes you can't know what you're made to do until you can't find what you're looking for anywhere else. In Henry Beston, she discovered a flat, featureless, and spiritless account of creation that could never do justice to the glorious globe that's spinning a thousand miles an hour underneath our feet. It was that lifeless book, ironically, that called to her as Jesus called to the already decaying Lazarus, "Come forth" (John 11:1–44 KJV). It felt like that "Come forth!" moment for Annie, snapping her imagination to attention and rousing her to write words that make the human heart race. Nobody out there seemed to be writing the kind of book Dillard was looking for, so she wrote it *herself*. She discovered a gap, a vacuum, an opening, and she filled it.

The book she wrote in response to Beston's boring memoir won the Pulitzer Prize the very next year! The book was called *Pilgrim at Tinker Creek*, and Annie was twenty-nine when she wrote it.

For the past fifty years, Annie has kept at it. But what has she been saying all this time?

"Waking Up" to the World

About *Pilgrim at Tinker Creek*, Diana Saverin wrote, "The book raises questions about the horrors and beauties of nature, and the power of the present moment in a world that's *constantly being created*" (emphasis added).[6] Scripture tells us that God is the Creator, sure, and theologians have long insisted that God is not a sheer static force of divinity. No, God is *alive*, they say, which is to say that God is *trinitarian*—Father, Son, and Holy Spirit—an interrelated web of dynamic relationship, a community of holy communion. And if God *is* the living and wildly alive Creator, his world must be, to borrow Saverin's phrase, "constantly being created."

And if it's true that the world is not just something that *was* created in the ancient past but indeed something that is *being created right now* by the very Spirit of God, then we had better stay awake and live alert. This is what Dillard has built her entire career upon—wakefulness, wonder, watching the world to see what happens next. But many people are taken aback and caught off guard when they discover how she goes about calling us to wakefulness. She finds the smallest creatures and the smallest details tucked away in the smallest dusty corners of creation—even the corners of our consciousness—and puts them on full display. She is the mistress of the mundane.

One of her highly acclaimed stories is "The Death of the Moth." It came to her while she was camping alone in the Blue Ridge Mountains of Virginia. It's a longer section, but it will help us see what wakefulness looks like.

One night a moth flew into the candle, was caught, burned dry, and held. I must have been staring at the candle, or maybe I looked up when a shadow crossed my page; at any rate, I saw it all. A golden female moth, a biggish one with a two-inch wingspan, flapped into the fire, dropped her abdomen into the wet wax, stuck, flamed, frazzled, and fried in a second. Her moving wings ignited like tissue paper, enlarging the circle of light in the clearing and creating out of the darkness the sudden blue sleeves of my sweater, the green leaves of jewelweed by my side, the ragged red trunk of a pine. At once the light contracted again and the moth's wings vanished in a fine, foul smoke. At the same time her six legs clawed, curled, blackened, and ceased, disappearing utterly. And her head jerked in spasms, making a spattering noise; her antennae crisped and burned away, and her heaving mouth parts crackled like pistol fire. When it was all over, her head was, so far as I could determine, gone, gone the long way of her wings and legs. Had she been new, or old? Had she mated and laid her eggs, had she done her work? All that was left was the glowing horn shell of her abdomen and thorax—a fraying, partially collapsed gold tube jammed upright in the candle's round pool.

And then this moth-essence, this spectacular skeleton, began to act as a wick. She kept burning. The wax rose in the moth's body from her soaking abdomen to her thorax to the jagged hole where her head should be, and widened into flame, a saffron-yellow flame that robed her to the ground like any immolating monk.[7]

But pay attention to the title of this story. She didn't title it "The Death of *a* Moth." No, that would have been too generic for Dillard. This story is rightly called "The Death of *the* Moth," and it's written as if this were the *only* moth ever to have lived and flapped and fluttered and flown into the fire of a tiny wicked candle. Something that happens a zillion times a year all over the world—a moth bedecked in flames—takes on a newness, carries a vividness. Here Dillard eulogizes a creature that came into her awareness only minutes before. And she writes a little seven-word sentence that lashes with force: "At any rate, *I saw it all.*"

It may seem like Dillard's writing is superfluous. It may seem like the painstaking detail she goes into is unnecessary, even wasteful. You may think, *How does anyone have that kind of time to* waste *on such unnecessary information? What does an immolating moth have to do with anything?* But that would precisely be missing the point. The entire point of Annie's work is to teach us to *notice*; to *see*; to *pay attention to the details* of our lives, the neighborhoods in which we live, and the subplots of the stories of the saints and sinners with whom we're traveling the road of life.

This is the essence of Dillard's writing. Seeing. Noticing. Hallowing the everyday experiences that the majority of us so regularly miss. She is a sort of ophthalmologist of the soul, diagnosing our blurred vision and fitting us with new lenses that open new worlds to us. She is a sort of cartographer of the realm of the senses, mapping the terrain, introducing us to the significant landmarks that we've walked by a thousand times unawares. She shakes us out of our haphazard haziness and shows us what's always been there. One literary critic said, "There is no way to avoid *seeing* again after you have read Annie Dillard."[8] She is a modern-day mystic, a perceiver, a re-enchanter of the world. All of which, I think, is exactly what we need in our screen-saturated society. Look up, says Annie Dillard, and see. See it *all*.

Turning Humdrum Neighborhoods into Holy Ground

If we had the time, we could take pen and paper and jot out a long genealogy of famous nature writers. John Muir, like an ancient Middle Eastern bedouin, roamed America's national parks at the mercy of the elements. He famously slept in the wind-torn tops of Douglas firs in the midst of torrential storms. He made his home with gargantuan grizzlies and hulking bull moose. And he reported back from the field.

He was a more unregenerate John the Baptist–like figure, a voice of one crying out in the wilderness. But Muir didn't come out of nowhere. His work was begotten by people like Henry David Thoreau, the famous naturalist and author of *Walden* who became known as one of the founding fathers of present-day environmentalism and called people to return to the land. So how does Annie Dillard stand out as remarkable among this fruitful family tree of naturalists?

Most nature writers have made a living by *fleeing* the suffocating confines of the city and the seeming sterility of suburban life to find meaning in the wilderness. They had to *leave home* to do their work. It would seem by their escape that holiness and mystery and exultant wonder are found in the hills and hinterlands. But that's not what we learn from Dillard. No, Annie Dillard won a Pulitzer Prize because she had an imagination vivid enough to turn suburbia into holy ground.

As *Pilgrim at Tinker Creek* made its initial pilgrimage into the world, people received it as a sort of monastic missive from the American wilds. They thought Dillard was writing from the edge of civilization or from an elevated and enlightened vista overlooking all the small, simple people living humdrum lives in unholy places. But they were dead wrong.

Over the years, people were shocked to discover that Dillard wrote the book as she sat by a creek in the middle of a bustling suburb in Roanoke, Virginia. In every direction, she could hear the sound of school buses stopping to pick up rambunctious children, fire trucks racing to put out adolescent flames, and ambulances hurrying to get oxygen to an elderly woman who would be fine but for the moment was experiencing a complication with her COPD. These sounds were a part of the cacophonous choir that filled Dillard's Tinker Creek sanctuary.

There were shopkeepers and tax accountants taking lunchtime walks around the creek. There were construction workers on union-sanctioned smoke breaks, standing in a corner of the park. Annie Dillard was writing from the middle of the mayhem, and she walked back home every evening to her small place on a crowded street. The unexpected genius of Dillard's Pulitzer Prize–winning book is her grounding in the actual conditions of everyday life.

This is a recurring theme in her life and work. A 1992 *New York Times* article tells it quite well:

> Annie Dillard was giving a reading on Cape Cod, Mass.,
> where she has a summer house. The house is in an area
> neither fashionable nor thick with writers, conditions that
> are nowadays often synonymous. During the question
> period a member of the audience rose on trembling legs
> and asked, "But why South Wellfleet?" Her manner—
> timid, awed—was appropriate to a shepherd's asking,
> "But why Bethlehem?"[9]

Speaking of the man from Bethlehem, in the most iconic prayer ever prayed, Jesus taught his disciples—and by extension, he taught *us*—to pray "Hallowed be thy name" (Matthew 6:9 KJV). The Greek word *hagiazō*, which we often translate "hallowed," means "to make or to render holy, to venerate or revere."[10] The very next phrase that Jesus supplied to the supplicants has at the end of it "in earth, as it is in heaven" (v. 10 KJV). "Hallowed be thy name . . . in earth, as it is in heaven." Stitch these sentences together and what you get is a prayer that aches for the beauty of God's name to get worked out in the very real conditions of our lives. The holiness of God invading the unholy streets.

In short, the praying people of God are called to participate in the resanctification of creation by welcoming and making space for the name of God. To make up a word, we Christians are called to the *re-holy-ing* of the world. Annie Dillard had the imaginative capacity to make the suburban streets of Roanoke into a mythical realm. As a student of Thoreau, she believed him when he said, "Heaven is under our feet as well as over our heads."[11]

Reading Dillard can be our awakening to the glory that is everywhere hiding in plain sight. Can you see it in the suburban neighborhood? Can you feel the crackling thunder of Mount Sinai in the kindergarten carpool line? Can you see Jesus in the little baby wrapped in swaddling clothes, lying in the tiny bassinette beside your bed, ready to rouse you through every watch of the night for a few calories of breast milk? Have you ever tripped over Jacob's ladder (Genesis 28:12), ever been caught in the crossfire between heaven and earth, ever heard the song of the angels that are always ascending and descending among us? We get tired and our eyes grow faint, but it's all right there, says Dillard. Can you *see* it?

We are much like the naturalist writers of the last couple of hundred years. We think we have to run from our seemingly shallow and underwhelming lives to find deeper meaning. We feel as if we have to flee the suffocating confines of the city and the seeming sterility of suburban life to make a meaningful contribution. But Dillard stands as a rebuke to all such Christian versions of escapism. To be faithful Christians, we have to be like Christ Jesus. And to be like Christ Jesus we have to run *into*, not *away from*, the small and insignificant places like Nazareth and Roanoke and Reno.

> To be like Christ Jesus we have to run *into*, not *away from*, the small and insignificant places like Nazareth and Roanoke and Reno.

The apostle John said it this way, as translated by Eugene H. Peterson: "The Word became flesh and blood, and moved into the neighborhood" (John 1:14 THE MESSAGE). To be faithful Christians requires the necessary death of our un-Christian escapism. Dillard wrote, "Beauty and grace are performed whether or not we . . . sense them. The least we can do is try to be there."[12]

This remarkable woman had the imaginative capacity to make the suburban streets of Roanoke, Virginia, into a mythical realm. And the question for us is this: Will we do the same with our own places? Will we do the hard work of transforming our own humdrum neighborhoods into holy ground?

Keeping the Windows Open on Another World

George Arthur Buttrick, one of the great preachers of the twentieth century, wrote a compelling story.

In a kindling book about prayer, E. Herman has reminded us of the story of "The Nun from Lyons." She was dancing at a fashionable ball. None was gayer or lovelier: her marriage to the most eligible man of her set was due within a week. Suddenly, in the midst of a minuet, she saw the vision of the world dying—for lack of prayer. She could almost hear the world's gasping, as a drowning man gasps for air. The dance now seemed macabre, a dance of death. In the corner a priest, smiling and satisfied, discussed the eligibles with a matchmaking mother: even the Church did not know that the world was dying—for want of prayer. As instant as a leaping altar flame, she vowed her life to ceaseless intercession, and none could dissuade her. She founded a contemplative order of prayer—lest the world should die. Was she quite wrong? Was she wrong at all? Or is our world saved by those who keep the windows open on another World?[13]

Reading this story—the story of a fashionable fiancée at a ball who, in a moment, renounced it all and became a nun—reminds me of Annie Dillard, who came from wealth, the daughter of a successful business executive, with access to education and every opportunity a girl could ask for. She could have chosen a conventional, unimaginative life of ease. She could have chosen the country club and never given herself over to the mysteries of Tinker Creek. But a conversion happened in her, a conversion from which she never recovered. It was a conversion that irreversibly threw open the windows to another world.

In a world of dull technologists and flat literalists and

market analysts, Annie Dillard has lived as a mystic. Like the nun from Lyons, her life has been a prayer of intercession, a prayer for the preservation of the world. And her writing has been a prayer of intercession *for us*, her readers. On every page she prays in the Spirit that we'll avoid the cheap shortcuts of a conventional and unimaginative life, prays that we'll be converted, that we'll always keep the windows open to another world.

Annie Dillard is a modern-day mystic. At the burning bush, Moses carried himself with a holy reticence, which is completely understandable. But I think Dillard would have stuck her face in the burning bush to see what was in there, even if it meant she would be burned and transfigured. And some of you may be wondering what you can learn from a figure that seems so strange and esoteric: *What can Annie Dillard do for me?* I'm glad you asked!

Dillard can help nurture the inner mystic within you, within all of us. And it is worth noting that "there are . . . a significant number of key thinkers in the Christian tradition, Rowan Williams and Karl Rahner being but two examples, who have argued for the renewal of mystical consciousness as a prerequisite for the survival of Christianity."[14] What a statement that Christianity will survive and make its unique contribution to the world only as long as its adherents live as mystics.

You may be a stay-at-home mom, changing diapers and working around nap schedules and fixing mac and cheese in what feels like an endless monotony. But Saint Annie Dillard wants you to know that there's mystery playing out all around you if you'll only have the eyes to see it. Like the young mother Mary who "treasured up all these things and pondered them in her heart" (Luke 2:19) as she stared at the young Christ child lying next to her, asleep in the manger, you can keep a window open on another world during those young toddler years! And you may be glad to know that Dillard wrote this book as a young housewife. While writing *Pilgrim at Tinker Creek*, she scribbled in her journal, depressed, wondering who would ever care to read a book written by a "Virginia housewife named Annie." The next year, her book won the Pulitzer Prize! That Virginia housewife changed the world indeed.

You may be a master electrician, but Annie Dillard wants you to know you can *also* be a mystic. As you travel from job to job, you can show up as a missionary of kindness and mercy in a world of crass construction workers. You can work with your eyes wide open to what's happening in the invisible realm of the Spirit. You can live a life of prayer and probing curiosity.

Everywhere you are is sacred. And if you will be there, living with holy wakefulness in a world that is "constantly being created" by the Spirit, paying attention to the invisible mysteries, and looking for the hidden beauty, your little section of the world will be saved!

> Everywhere you are is sacred.

We need more Annie Dillards. Which is to say, we need more everyday mystics who see their places for what they are: holy ground!

PART III

THE *PRACTICES* OF STABILITY IN PLACE

A BRIEF INTERLUDE

We Need Holy Practices

IN PART I (CHAPTERS 1–3) WE LOOKED AT THE *POWER* of stability in place, learned about the ancient vow the saints took, and discovered the God-given purpose of place—to give us security, identity, and meaningful work through which we can exercise skilled mastery in God's good world.

In part II (chapters 4–7) we paid attention to the *principles* of stability in place. We discussed the membership benefits of place, acknowledged that people are the great purifiers, thought through what our skills can do for our particular places, and named the reality that wherever we find ourselves living can be hallowed as holy ground. To purify and provoke our imaginations, we gleaned from the examples of saints and sages who have lived lives of stability in place.

In part III (chapters 8–13) it's time to ask, How do we live out the vow of stability? My contention is that stability is not an abstract concept. Stability is not a spiritual gift that comes naturally to certain people. Stability does not descend from the heavens. Stability is as concrete as our daily routines, as strong as the relationships we pour ourselves into, as deep as the community we become members of, and as stable as the institutions we give ourselves over to. And because of that reality, I'm going to put in front of you five pathways—*five holy practices*—that can play an integral part in the realization of rootedness in our local places. They are the practices of stability in *home*, stability in *family*, stability in *friendship*, stability in *church*, and stability in *community*.

These chapters will be succinct and will move quickly. They are meant to throw open doors and inspire imaginative possibilities about the place you live that you might not have considered yet. Or maybe they will remind you of practices you've engaged in the past that are calling for a recommitment.

So mark up the margins of these chapters. And consider how you can start developing new disciplines that will deepen your roots of stability in your present place.

CHAPTER 8

STABILITY IN HOME

Anywhere—and, it follows, nowhere—can be a
place. As long as we are there, to think and talk,
to listen and respond. The world, once conscious
of itself in the form of human making, is a vast
concert hall. What sounds there is not the divine
music of celestial spheres, as the ancient Greek
mathematicians believed, but the sound of one
human after another issuing the daily plea: to be
heard, to be understood, to be accommodated.

—*Mark Kingwell*

LISA AND I HAD BEEN MARRIED FOR TWELVE DAYS when we packed up everything we owned and threw it into the back of a bright yellow Penske truck. By "everything we owned" I mean a few mismatched pieces of furniture from our parents' homes, our clothes, our books, some dishes and cups and fine china, and a new gas grill our friends bought us as a wedding gift. We were moving from Tulsa, Oklahoma, which was the only place I had ever lived, to Colorado Springs to start our new life together. I had been hired to be a pastor at New Life Church, and Lisa had been hired to teach sixth graders at a charter school.

Up to this point, Lisa had only visited Colorado Springs a few short days, and I had only lived there during a three-month summer internship. We had very little knowledge of the city and even less money, so I flew out by myself a couple of months before the wedding to find our first apartment. I scoured the city and found one and secured it by paying the first month's rent. Then I flew back to Tulsa to get ready for the wedding and the impending move to Colorado.

You can imagine the low-grade anxiety I carried that whole twelve-hour Penske ride from Tulsa to Colorado Springs. Lisa would be seeing the apartment *for the first time* when we arrived, and to make the stakes even higher, both sets of our parents were caravanning with us to help us get settled. I thought, *What if they don't like it? What if they think it's a piece of trash?* Mercifully, when we arrived, both Lisa *and* our parents were thrilled! It was simple and small, of course, but it was clean and had a fresh coat of paint. We had a great few days getting things moved in and showing our parents around town, and then they drove back to Tulsa. It was just Lisa and me now.

On Monday morning, we both got up early and got ready for the first day at our new jobs. We had one vehicle, so I drove Lisa to the school and dropped her off. I kissed her, and then she got out of the car with her bag of lesson plans and school supplies and a sack lunch that we packed together. I'll never forget watching that smart, stunning twenty-four-year-old woman walk into the building. Then I drove to the church and carried in a box of books and my own sack lunch to get started at my first real job after college. I was twenty-two. *Here we go!* I thought. Our whole lives had been building to this moment. And now it was time to start building a life together. But I was about to learn one of the first and most basic steps you have to take to start building a life.

Making a Home as an Act of Creation

I picked Lisa up after our first full day of work, and we came back to our apartment. It was just after 5:00 p.m., and we were tired and hungry, so we started making dinner. It was a simple meal—chicken and rice with a salad on the side, as I recall—and we sat at our table, just the two of us, for the first time. We talked about our work and the new people we had met, and there was joy. When we were done, we cleaned up the table and washed the dishes. And when the dried dishes were placed back in the cupboard, I watched something like a sacred switch that flipped on in Lisa.

She started walking around the apartment, looking at what needed to be done to make the place feel like home. She got out a measuring tape to see how long the walls were. She was envisioning what kind of artwork needed to hang over the couch in our small living room. She walked the tiny spaces to feel the dimensions under her feet. Where should a coffee table go? And where should we put the two plants she had in mind? Somehow Lisa knew that a fiddle-leaf fig and a western African snake plant would make this little ten-by-fifteen room pop with all their green goodness. I had never even heard of these plants, but that didn't matter—she was scribbling down notes on a legal pad. Time stood still as I watched her. This woman who had been my wife for all of seventeen days had been transfigured into a sort of mythical figure. She knew what she was doing, and all I could do was stand in awe—and stand out of her way—as her genius expressed itself.

We went to a few different shops and stores over the next week and got what we needed. Soon enough, the empty apartment was gorgeous and homey and thriving on our thrift-store budget. On a weekly basis, people gathered around our table for good food and fun games, for conversation that became camaraderie in our new workplaces. Lisa even had fifteen of her students over for enchiladas and dessert after they met a lofty reading goal.

In my uncultured twenty-two-year-old mind, I would

never have thought to spend a little bit of time and a little bit of money to make an apartment beautiful. I knew we were passing through. I knew we had signed a one-year lease on a place that we would leave in our dust. I saw cheap drywall with decent paint. I saw someone else's place that we were borrowing for twelve months. But Lisa knew it would be the place we would host family and friends for their visits to Colorado Springs. In her mind's eye she saw our new neighbors and coworkers and friends from church sitting at our kitchen table, sharing their hearts and their joys, sharing their fears and their tears. And for people to do that, Lisa knew it had to feel like a *home*. It had to be a place where people wanted to be, and it would feel that way only if *we* wanted to be in it. All I could see in our apartment was *impermanence*. But Lisa saw the place we would call home for the first year of our lives together, the place where we'd make our earliest memories as a married couple, a place that could become *home* if we would only do the work of *treating* it like home.

In that first year of our marriage, Lisa taught me "the art of placemaking."[1] She taught me how to turn a generic, drab space into a particularly beautiful place. She showed me how to make a home out of a temporary apartment. It wasn't going to be ours long term, but it *became* ours for that year. And I have since come to believe that it's hard to start building a life in a new place—a

> It's hard to start building a life in a new place . . . when you haven't first done the work of cultivating your own little homeplace *in which* and *from which* to live that life.

new city, a new community—when you haven't first done the work of cultivating your own little homeplace *in which* and *from which* to live that life.

The First Economy

In many parts of the world, the daily news cycle hums with numbers and figures, stock filings and economic forecasts. Depending on how the Dow Jones Industrial Average closed today, we'll know if we're keeping up with the Joneses. The ticker at the bottom of the television tells us that Tesla is up 10 percent over yesterday! A new interview with Warren Buffett is aired, and we find out what the Oracle of Omaha is thinking so we can know how to think about our stake in the world, no matter how small it might be. But the brilliant Jeffrey Bilbro, a professor of English, reminds us that while "the word *economy* calls up lists of statistics and numbers," we are wise to "remember . . . that the word *economy* comes from the Greek word *oikos*, which means household."[2]

Economy, in the ancient mind, didn't first flag thoughts of an abstract market, a national jobs report, or a gross domestic product. To care about matters of economy was to care about the homeplace and its semblance of order, to care about the state of the fences and the gate that closed in the livestock. Were they strong and secure? Would they keep the right stuff in and the wrong stuff out? To care about the economy was to care about the upkeep of the small house in which you were living. Were the seams of boards well sealed from the outside? Would you be able to withstand the winter in this place? To care about the economy was to care about housing your aging parents and the learning opportunities your place would afford the children. Education for them wasn't about learning facts and historical dates and abstract math and interesting scientific data for the sake of test scores; education was the acquisition of deep knowledge and useful skills that would be applied to a new trade that could support them into the future. If you had these things, you were living in a strong economy. In short, the *household*, the *homeplace*, the *place that you and your people live*, was the smallest concentric circle of well-being and thus needed to be tended to *first*.

Now, of course, most of us are not agrarians and do not live as agrarians. I understand that. But I don't think you need to be one for this economy principle to hold. You don't need to be a farmer or a rancher to care about preserving the orderliness of the place you live. Many of you are homeschoolers, and so much of your life plays out in your place. Have you given thoughtful consideration to how your place needs to be organized for your people to thrive? Many of you are business owners and work from your home. Have you structured your place so you have a dedicated and sane workstation for your workday while still being able to walk away from work at night and experience home? Many of you have shops or warehouses attached to your home, with construction equipment that needs to be tended and kept in good order. They are to you what livestock is to a rancher— they keep you supplied; they are the way you pay your bills. So have you turned your place into holy ground?

I think we could stand to recover the household as the

first economy. Home is not just a roof over our heads, though that is a great gift in itself. Home is a haven from which we rise rested to launch out into the world with God's blessing, and it is the place we run back to so as to recover after a good day's work. It is the place where memories are made and futures are formed. It is the place where imaginations are sparked and lifelong relationships are solidified. It is the place we learn to pray, and it should be the place where it's safe to weep.

So do your best to make your household holy ground. Hang pictures on the walls. Paint it with colors that bring you joy. Work to create order and orderliness. You may be in a college dorm, you may be renting a room in someone's basement, you may be holed up in a cramped apartment that you hope is temporary—wherever you are, find ways to make it *yours* for the time you're there.

CHAPTER 9

STABILITY IN FAMILY

The family is one of nature's masterpieces.
—*George Santayana*

AS LONG AS EVERYTHING'S OKAY AT 10705 SOUTH
Eighty-Fifth East Avenue, nothing else really matters.
Every family has its important sayings, key phrases, and pithy statements that sustain them through the years. They act as a sort of thermostat, adjusting the temperature of a family's culture when love is frigid and hope has grown cold. The opening statement in this chapter has been one of ours for all of my life. It was birthed in a season of great trial for my parents.

They had four young kids, and their work at our local church was bewildering. A guest speaker was sowing doctrinal division within the church that was separating people, and their hearts were broken. One night my parents had tucked us, their four little ones, into bed. They were exhausted, and after bedtime prayers my mom collapsed on the couch, weeping and wondering when relief would come. My dad sat down next to her, scooped her into his arms, and that family-shaping, culture-defining statement came out of him: "As long as everything's okay at 10705 South Eighty-Fifth East Avenue, nothing else really matters." And as a family, we haven't stopped saying it since.

Now, of course, they didn't mean that literally. They didn't mean to suggest that our neighbors could be suffering next door, in want of food and aching for friendship, but as long as everything's okay at our place, we could ignore them. They didn't intend to communicate that our family is the center of the universe. What they meant was that there will be times when a threat arises and our family is tested. They understood that in those times a decision would have to be made: we will either crumble under the pressure and let someone else's toxicity destroy us, or we will pull together and care for one another *through* those trials until we come out on the other side. In those times, there will be plenty that we cannot control, but there is one thing we *can* control: we *can* decide to love one another, to serve one another, to be gracious with one another. In short, we can choose to be a *family*.

It turns out that Toni Morrison, the first black woman to win the Nobel Prize in literature, shared some of these defining statements within her own family. Like my parents, Toni was in a particularly difficult stretch at work. Her aging father was in the kitchen, drinking his morning coffee, when she opened up to him. In an essay for the *New Yorker*, Toni told the story:

> One day, alone in the kitchen with my father, I let drop a few whines about the job. I gave him details, examples of what troubled me, yet although he listened intently, I saw no sympathy in his eyes. . . . Perhaps he understood that what I wanted was a solution to the job, not an escape from it. In any case, he put down his cup of coffee and said, "Listen. You don't live there. You live here. With your people. Go to work. Get your money. And come on home."

That was what he said. This was what I heard:

1. Whatever the work is, do it well—not for the boss but for yourself.
2. You make the job; it doesn't make you.
3. Your real life is with us, your family.
4. You are not the work you do; you are the person you are.

I have worked for all sorts of people since then, geniuses and morons, quick-witted and dull, bighearted and narrow. I've had many kinds of jobs, but since that conversation with my father I have never considered the level of labor to be the measure of myself, and I have never placed the security of a job above the value of home.[1]

Her father's profound wisdom still simmers on the page: "Listen. You don't live there. You live here. *With your people.* Go to work. Get your money. And *come on home.*"

This was a man who grew up in the sweltering wasteland of American racism. He knew what it was like to be abused and degraded and dehumanized. He knew what it was like to be trapped in systems that not only subjugated the body but also threatened the spirit and contaminated the soul. He *knew.* But he also wanted his daughter to know that while she would have to interact with foolish and stupid and mean-spirited people from time to time, she would always be able to *come home* to the sanctuary of her relatives—to the people who were born into a common blood covenant to care for one another and to work to repair one another, scrubbing out the infection inflicted in the workplace and the larger world.

Morrison wrote that since that conversation, "I have never placed the security of a job above the value of home."[2] And she also wrote about the mutual joy that comes when families live well together: "The pleasure of being *necessary* to my parents was profound."[3] She knew she needed her father's wisdom, but she also knew he needed her. *She was necessary to their meaning. They* were necessary to her formation and sense of protection. The mutual necessity of interfamily relations might be *the* remarkable quality of the institution of the family.

Four Postures That Lead to Stability in Family

As a pastor, I sit with people on a daily basis who report back to me from the field. I understand not all families function this way and not all families are a safe place. I grieve with all of you who live insecurely around your kin, and I pray you can be a part of establishing for future generations what you don't yet have. As part of that, I want to offer some postures for you to consider that could lead to the creation of stability within your family.

1. *Listen.* Do you know how desperate people are to share their hearts? Do you know how isolating it can feel not to be able to say the thing that scares you? Of course you do! Which is why listening to your family members is a monumental matter. Ask good questions to draw out the depths of the people you love. Be direct by saying to your family that there's

nothing that's off-limits to say. Often the soul-ache we carry is a result of being stopped up emotionally. But sharing with someone who knows how to listen can unclog the soul.

2. *Learn.* Every person is uniquely crafted by God. There are no formulas, no molds. There is only mystery when you're dealing with a creature created in the image of God. So develop a posture of attentiveness to your family members. Learn about them, their unique giftings, their interesting quirks, and the intricacies of their making. And do it without judgment. Become a student of your most important people.

> Become a student of your most important people.

3. *Leverage.* We all have distinct skills and particular proficiencies. You, the listener and the learner, have the opportunity to leverage your skills for the strengthening of your family members. Give them the very best of your giftings. You can't do everything, but with what you can do, do it with all your heart for the sake of their good!

4. *Love.* Make the simple commitment to love your people till death, because these are the people God gave you, and God gave you to them. They will make mistakes. But so will you. Be quick to forgive one another. "Love covers over a multitude of sins" (1 Peter 4:8). Give them the affirmation that God the Father gave God the Son: "You are my Son, whom I love; with you I am well pleased" (Mark 1:11). Walk the long road of love with your people.

THE POWER OF PLACE

Stability in Marriage

Speaking of "till death do us part," let's talk about one of the most significant ancient Christian practices that can help us plant our lives firmly: the practice of marriage. But what is marriage anyway?

In the whirlwind of this information age, amid a glut of Netflix narratives, we have been inundated with marital misinformation. The writer of the book of Hebrews says, "Let marriage be held in honor among all" (13:4 ESV). But marriage in many cases has been reduced to a social norm for those looking to settle down, a conjugal arrangement, a yearly tax benefit, something you resort to with your live-in partner to get your old-fashioned parents off your back, a cheap contractual agreement that can be torn up when the two parties are ready to move on to their next adventure. Marriage is now something from which sophisticated celebrities and iconic singer-songwriters "consciously uncouple."[4]

A popular magazine and website founded by actress Gwyneth Paltrow has an article that cites the 50 percent divorce rate in the United States and ties it to increased life expectancies. The thinking goes: we humans used to live much shorter lives, so people only had time for one marriage, but now we're living longer and that's exposing that we either *can't* last that long with one person or *weren't made to* last that long with one person.[5] The article's authors say that divorce is only a problem *in our minds*; it's a problem because we're too rigid with our forms and practices and too limited in our thinking. We aren't yet enlightened enough to realize just how disposable marriage should be. They go on to say:

> To put it plainly, as divorce rates indicate, human beings haven't been able to fully adapt to our skyrocketing life expectancy. Our biology and psychology aren't set up to be with one person for four, five, or six decades. . . .
>
> The idea of being married to one person for life, especially without some level of awareness of our unresolved emotional needs, is too much pressure for anyone. . . .
>
> The high divorce rate might actually be a calling to learn a new way of being in relationships.[6]

Thus, for these authors, conscious uncoupling is the reasonable way forward. They are telling us a new day is here. They want us to adjust.

Of course, divorces are going to happen. As a pastor, I have sat and wept with ailing couples in living rooms and in courtrooms. I am no cold-blooded idealist. I am no finger-pointing man of the cloth. "In this world you will have trouble," said Jesus (John 16:33). And, boy, was he right! The trouble sometimes comes from the outside, from those seeking to destroy our lives. But the trouble also comes from inside the home, with our own actions serving as the destroyer.

Moses pastored people who walked through the wilderness of divorce. Jesus didn't get out of talking about it with conflicted couples either. Life on planet Earth is precarious, dangerous, wild.

And *still*, there's more.

And *still*, in the midst of the pastoral counsel of Moses and the prophetic witness of Jesus, in the midst of cultural accretions and attempted matrimonial redefinitions, the church has been saying "till death do us part" for centuries. That's because the church has always had a high view of marriage.

In the fourth century, John Chrysostom called the home, newly created in the marriage covenant, the "small church."[7] In the exchanging of vows, the husband and the wife were anointed by the Spirit of God to be the established priesthood of this church-in-miniature, the redeemed Adam and Eve, building a particular place of worship on planet Earth. In this tiny home sanctuary, prayers would be prayed, hands would be raised—not against each other but to the heavens—the foundations of discipleship would be laid. And from it the world would be changed. The home was understood to be a microcosm of the primordial garden of Eden, the place where everyone, working to live in harmony, could learn to walk with God "in the cool of the day" (Genesis 3:8).

In Eastern Orthodox marriage services, there is a crowning ritual that serves as the centerpiece of the ceremony. Crowns are fashioned out of garland wreaths or orange blossoms or myrtle leaves, and the priest places them on the heads of the bride and the groom. The crowns are tied together by a white ribbon, signifying purity and unity. And all this is meant to be a sort of coronation of the wife and the husband, now ruling together as queen and king of this new domain. But the crowns they wear are like the crowns of the martyrs in Revelation 2:10. They now have been endowed from on high with the power to give their lives for each other. Rather than consciously uncoupling when things get difficult, Christians have been called to become like Jesus, and to live into the covenant marriage that Jesus shares with his bride, the church—a communion sealed in blood and enlivened by a broken body.

Yes, the writer of the book of Hebrews says, "Let marriage be held in honor among all" (13:4 ESV), because any place where such love and loyalty and fidelity are practiced deserves deep respect.

The Reasons People Leave

So why do we keep walking away? What are the existential threats to stability in marriage?

First, at the most fundamental level, we leave because of *bad manners*. John M. Gottman has spent fifty years as a psychologist, clinician, and researcher of marital stability. He has come up with a list of divorce predictors known as "the Four Horsemen of the Apocalypse [that] clip-clop into the heart of marriage: criticism, contempt, defensiveness and stonewalling."[8] It's not that complicated. Bad manners over a stretch of time begin to function like a pickax, chipping away at emotional connection and disintegrating intimacy. The little stuff accrues a negative compounding interest over the years and becomes the big stuff.

But second, and even more damaging than Gottman's four horsemen, we have *faulty assumptions* and *unrealistic expectations*. Theologian and ethicist Stanley Hauerwas observed:

Destructive to marriage is the self-fulfillment ethic that assumes marriage and the family are primarily institutions of personal fulfillment, necessary for us to become "whole" and happy. The assumption is that there is someone just right for us to marry and that if we look closely enough, we will find the right person. This moral assumption overlooks a crucial aspect to marriage. It fails to appreciate the fact that *we always marry the wrong person*. We never know whom we marry; we just think we do. Or even if we first marry the right person, just give it a while and he or she will change. For marriage, being [the enormous thing it is], means we are not the same person after we have entered it. The primary problem is . . . learning how to love and care for the stranger to whom you find yourself married.[9] (emphasis added)

Is Hauerwas just some old curmudgeonly nihilist? There are people who feel God *led* them to their spouse. What are they to think about the statement that "we always marry the wrong person"? I think Hauerwas simply wants to name the fact that no matter who you marry, there is going to be conflict and frustration. He wants to name that, if you're going to be faithful to someone over the course of decades, it will take every bit of your resolve. Our patron saint of place, Wendell Berry, wrote, "There are no unsacred places; there are only sacred places and desecrated places."[10] The same could be said about marriages: there are no unsacred ones, only sacred or desecrated ones.

Hauerwas wants us to remember that if Jesus is our example, we shouldn't be surprised if marriage sometimes takes the shape of a cross. He wants us to remember that a good marriage is like a good story, and anyone who knows anything about a good story knows that it will have plot twists into the absurd and melancholic, it will meet seemingly insurmountable odds, and the musical score may sometimes shift from moments of major happiness into a minor key of misery.

Hauerwas wants to challenge the cultural assumption that marriage is primarily about someone else bringing *me* fulfillment. He wants to challenge the belief that broken parts of us automatically become whole when joined to another person. I have officiated nearly one hundred weddings after counseling each couple for months. From time to time I have seen people with major gaps in their character think that marrying someone else would help fill in those gaps. I can tell you authoritatively that marriage does not. Sometimes it even exacerbates them.

Reading back over Hauerwas's paragraph, I can hardly think of an idea more diametrically opposed to the modern-day gospel of conscious uncoupling. The unholy priests who so quickly propagate separation and divorce when things get difficult will find this to be a hard word from Dr. Hauerwas. The task, the call, the holy vocation of holy matrimony is to learn how to serve another who sees the world differently. The task is to deny yourself, take up your cross, and follow Jesus up the hill, even if—and maybe especially *when*—it hurts like hell. Marriage is like a crucible that can form Christlikeness in us if we will let it.

And third, marriages are threatened by *lust*. In his fourteenth-century descent into the *Inferno* of hell,

Dante Alighieri is taken deep into the realm of lust. His tour guide, the ancient Roman poet Virgil, describes lust as a tormentor.

> To this torment [the torment of lust] are condemned the carnal damned. Those for whom desire conquered reason.[11]

Unchecked desire indeed conquers reason. Untamed desire blinds us to the beauty in front of us. Darkened desire drives us to leave home in search of the very gift we have just left behind. Dante's understanding of lust is among the more prescient portrayals in the last seven hundred years. In his vision of hell, lust is like a violent tornadic vortex that sucks a person into a funnel cloud of infidelity. When trapped in the cloud, one cannot *stay* anywhere. He is blown from place to place, leaving destruction everywhere he goes. Remember that this book in your hand, *The Power of Place*, is about reclaiming the vow of stability in a rootless age.

> The task, the call, the holy vocation of holy matrimony is to learn how to serve another who sees the world differently.

Fidelity in marriage is one of the primary practices that leads to stability. In contrast, lust institutionalizes a life of self-inflicted instability. Lust, after all, is sin. And all throughout Scripture, sin leads to exile. Lust, we could say, results in relational homelessness.

But *why*? Why is the sin of lust so disruptive? Because lust dissipates. It specializes in the diffusion of what could be a concentrated and thus substantial affection. Lust takes the loaf of bread that could feed a family and smashes it into a million crumbs, leaving everyone hungry. Lust is the lie that sole loyalty to the spouse of your vows is *constraining*. It tells us that we're missing out. Jesus knew this about lust, and so he didn't tiptoe around the topic. In the Sermon on the Mount, he was clear that adultery is not *only* a sexual act but a disposition of the heart that constantly undermines intimacy, fidelity, stability, and love (Matthew 5:27–29).

But these words of Jesus aren't directed just toward married people! At some point, all of us have been touched by and implicated in this. On some level, all of us have been guilty of adultery. The water is so polluted that we are not able to remember what clean water tasted like. Yes, we are living in a crisis of sexual impurity. The stats of those regularly watching pornography are mind-boggling. The accessibility of it is depressing. The hook-up culture that has become so common is like a tinderbox into which the match of our voracious desire has been thrown.

Who would have thought that faithful marriage could function as a sort of spiritual warfare against the principalities and powers that drive us into debilitating instability?

The Walls of Wonder

When I introduced you to the ancient vow of stability in chapter 2, I also introduced you to G. K. Chesterton and his concept of the walls of wonder.

The sacrament of marriage is an invitation into holy limitations. But we are living in the devastation of our own day: the walls have been knocked down and we have been exposed to the "naked peril of the precipice." The sexual boundaries that were meant to keep us safe, that were meant to preserve our song, have been disregarded. And so our souls have been silenced.

Millennia before Chesterton came along, Moses, the ancient Hebrew pastor and prophet, was one of the original wall builders. In the Ten Commandments, Moses gave us a blueprint from God on how to construct "a wall round the cliff's edge" so that we "could fling [our]selves into every frantic game" and make the world "the noisiest of nurseries." That is what the Ten Commandments serve as, after all—walls that keep us from wandering into the far country of infidelity.

One of the major sections of the wall is the seventh commandment: "You shall not commit adultery" (Exodus 20:14). But, sadly, too many read this primarily as a *prohibition* when they should be reading it as a *protection*. Too many people read it as God locking them *out* of a world of pleasure instead of God locking them *into* a rich and textured relationship that can lead to lifelong intimacy. And too many fail to realize that as we obey the seventh commandment, God is not just locking us into joy, he's also locking the devil out!

We have all witnessed a soon-to-be-groom at dinner with his garrulous groomsmen the night before the wedding. Inevitably, a stranger will walk over to their table, look at the groom, and say, "Hey, brother, enjoy your last night of freedom! Tomorrow begins the ball and chain." How anemic is their vision? How emaciated is their understanding? The holy union of two married people becomes a walled city, yes, but these are the walls of a playground, the walls of a fortified polis, not the walls of a prison yard.

There are ultimately two ways we can understand these matrimonial walls: as walls of *withholding* or walls of *wonder*. One way sees marriage as an entrapment, an impediment, as something that's keeping us from personal fulfillment. Many people think that God's primary objective is to block us from euphoria. He is the cosmic killjoy, giving us an arbitrary list of impossible commandments and random prohibitions. From the days in Eden, we humans have not trusted that God has our best interest in mind. Like Adam and Eve, we think God is *restraining* us when, in reality, he's *releasing* us into freedom. We run out to bemoan the fenced boundaries instead of enjoying the gift of life in the center of the garden. We see everything we *can't have* instead of rejoicing in everything that's *already ours*.

But the other way sees marriage as a sacred space wherein wonder is preserved, intimacy is protected, and love is nurtured. Many people see their spouse as the one treasured partner with whom they are privileged to share life's sojourn. They see the blessing in the enclosure. They see the multiplication in the limitation. The church and the world would be strengthened if more married couples saw themselves dwelling within the walls of wonder.

The Sacred Canopy

The book of Proverbs is a collection of accepted ancient wisdom distilled into pithy sayings. Just like the "as long as everything's okay" statement my parents passed on to me and my siblings. The proverbs are meant to be easy to memorize. And King Solomon and his officials wanted us to memorize them, to carry them with us. One of my favorites is Proverbs 14:26, and I remember memorizing it in middle school.

> Whoever fears the LORD has a secure fortress,
> *and for their children it will be a refuge.*
> (emphasis added)

Having studied how life works, Solomon acknowledges that our actions have consequences. For those who *refuse* to fear the Lord, pain and heartache and chaos are on the horizon. Solomon knew all about this, for he wrestled with profound bouts of waywardness. But he also knew that many would choose to fear the Lord and diagnosed what the result would be for them and their children: they would live a life of *refuge*.

This holy refuge has been one of the truest experiences of my life. And not because of anything I've done. I think of my maternal grandparents, Daniel and Weezie Wilson, who were married for nearly sixty-six years. They loved and honored each other, and their reputation was spotless after decades of serving people in their small town of 697 people. Their years of fearing the Lord continue to be a refuge for their five children, ten grandchildren, and twenty-three great-grandchildren. I think of my paternal grandparents, Melvin Joseph and Velma Ida Grothe, who worked hard every day of their lives and made sure my dad—their only child—grew up with deep integrity, a disciplined work ethic, and a love for the church. Their lives have served as a sort of sacred canopy under which my life has played out. I think of my parents, David and Becky Grothe, who have been married for forty-three years. I think of my in-laws, Larry and Linda Wakley, who have been married for fifty-one years. These are the four most important couples in my life, the people who brought me into this world and who have made my life possible.

They have lived for decades within the blessed walls of wonder. They know that boundaries lead to benediction. Their fidelity, their sincerity, and their integrity are the greatest treasures that Lisa and I have inherited. They have given us so very little to overcome and hardly anything to unlearn. Because of them, we find it easy to trust. Because of them, we feel secure and stable. Because of them, we have been protected from unnecessarily disastrous storms. Don't get me wrong, we've weathered plenty of storms. Life is hard enough. Pain finds us all. But their marriages have covered us, sheltered us, been a place for our lives to find respite in a dangerous world. Solomon hit the nail on the head: "Whoever fears the LORD has a secure fortress, *and for their children it will be a refuge.*"

Not many realize that marriage is one of the great pillars, one of the true institutions of a decent society. Yes, the union established by God in the beginning is meant to hold things together in a fractured world.

So if you find yourself married, remember that these walls are not meant to be the walls of a prison yard but of a playground. So live it up. Receive the gift in holy wonder.

Hold hands with your spouse and pray. Repent regularly. Forgive each other quickly. Make eye contact in a depersonalizing world. When the lies come to you that greater joy can be found elsewhere, rebuke them. You can be an agent of stability, a practicing member in the sustaining of the world.

But all of us, whether or not we're married, come from a family. We have people with whom we can practice stability. We have people for whom we can leverage our strength. We have people with whom we can share and receive love. We all have people we can listen to and learn about.

And when we are swept up in the madness of the world, we remember the words of Toni Morrison's dad: "Listen. You don't live there. You live here. *With your people.* Go to work. Get your money. And *come on home.*"

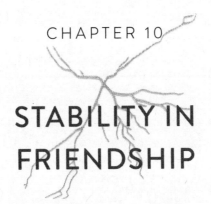

CHAPTER 10

STABILITY IN FRIENDSHIP

Adult friendship is two people saying, "I haven't seen you in forever; we should really hang out more" over and over again until one of you dies.

—*Anonymous*

A FRIEND OF MINE TOOK A JOB WORKING WITH A nongovernmental organization (NGO) deep in the bush of Africa. He was doing work that would sustainably supply clean water to a small tribe suffering from waterborne illnesses. But the work was long and required him to live with the tribe for nearly six months.

While he had some regular interaction with the women of the tribe, cultural and linguistic barriers made it more appropriate for him to spend most of his time with the men. The tribal chief, in particular, was his liaison. The chief had a decent grasp of English, as he was the one to communicate with the outside health organizations through the years.

One day, in his clapboard English, the chief said, "Tell me about the American man." My friend explained that the American man works a lot.

These African men, living in primitive conditions, were obviously used to a hard day's work, but they were shocked to hear that the American man has to leave his home, his closest people, and his immediate geographical space to do his work. Yes, my friend said, the American man is away from his home sometimes up to half a day (twelve hours), and when you factor in sleep (six to eight hours), he's only awake and with his family, his little tribe, for four to six hours a day. Being a commuter means he is in his car or on public transportation for long stretches of the day. And when he's in the office, very often he's sitting at a desk behind a computer screen, working as an individual in isolation. The longer my friend detailed the life of the American man, the more he felt as if he was digging a hole.

"But," my friend added, "maybe the one saving grace is that the American man makes pretty good money."

Without hesitation, the African chief said, "So the American man is *lonely*." It was a rhetorical statement, and the searing accuracy of it left my friend speechless.

Life for the members of the tribe was different. They worked together, and their children carried out the daily tasks with them. Even though they worked their fingers to the bone in a subsistence farming economy, the women were joyful and playful with one another. They had deep friendships. Meals were prepared and shared communally with conversations spilling into the night. Life for the tribe was intrinsically multigenerational, with grandparents sharing their ancestral stories and deep wisdom with all the children, and the children using their strength to serve the elderly. In short, they had "a 'thick' community in which people know and look out for one another and invest in relationships that are not transient."[1]

My friend initially thought he was going to Africa to help this tribe, but as these things normally go, the tribe ended up *helping him* by teaching him how to live. He came back and changed everything about his life. He got to work building routines that could lead to deeper friendships. He saw what the tribe had, and he didn't want to be one of those lonely American men.

The First Problem in the Bible

It takes reading only the first two chapters of the Bible to find the first problem. Before the crisis, creation cracks into coherence at the thundering command of God, and in Genesis 1 it tells us that seven times God saw that it was good. But you turn the page to Genesis 2, and, *boom*, there it is. God forms the man from the dust of the ground and breathes the breath of life into his nostrils. The man wakes up to wonder and then wonders what he ought to be doing. His first task is presented to him: name the animals. Adam gets right to it, exercising his masterful dominion within the animal kingdom. But something just isn't right.

> Then the LORD God said, "It is not good that the man should be alone." (Genesis 2:18 ESV)

Adam had meaningful *projects*. Adam had a gorgeous garden *place*. Adam had plenty of *provision*. But Adam did not ultimately have what he needed: a *person*, a companion, a *friend*. He did not have another image bearer with whom he could talk, share his heart, open up. To the people who well-meaningly say, "God is all I need," I present this story.

Adam had God all to himself, and *God* was the one who said, "It is *not good*." Something was missing. Which means that the first problem identified in the Bible is the problem of *loneliness*.

Now would be a good moment to say that you don't have to be married to be fulfilled. Single people often hear this passage preached in a way that creates unnecessary and unfortunate shame. They are made to feel that because they are not *married*, they are somehow missing out on *the fullness*, that their lives are interminably limited until their relational (mis)fortunes are reversed. No, no, no! The New Testament was a world-shattering document because Jesus and Paul and so many of the other major players presented a new paradigm: namely, that you can live in *the fullness* without being married. Jesus, himself a happily unmarried man, broadened the understanding of the family and gave us an invitation into the larger family of God.

Furthermore, readers of this passage might understand Eve narrowly, as simply Adam's *wife*, which conjures a very rigid role—namely, that of bearing children, of propagating the human race. Eve, of course, bore children. And yes, of course, that kept the human story going. But that reality can obscure the fact that Eve and Adam were *friends* first. They walked that beautiful garden and surely talked about the shimmering glory of the dew-drenched grass in the morning and the fading beauty of the sun that gives way to nightfall. They harvested and prepared meals that sprang up from the ground they tended together.

> Having friends means we never have to walk this weary planet alone.

Sadly, because our society oversexualizes everything, we all too quickly forget just how beautiful friendship is. Having friends means we never have to walk this weary planet alone. And the treasure of friendship is an inheritance God has provided for all of us. But many of us are living lives bereft of deep friendship.

A Theology of Friendship

I'll now make a claim that may seem strange to many of you. One of the greatest gifts the church can give to the world is her *theology of friendship*. But what do I mean by that?

First, have you ever been intrigued by the fact that Jesus often gathered a group of people around him? And it wasn't just the twelve disciples either. Jesus had a burgeoning community that he lived among and shared life with. Beyond the Twelve were Mary and Martha, sisters of Lazarus. Mary, the mother of Jesus, who probably became something of a de facto den mother to the extended group. And enough of a crew to send out seventy-two disciples, giving them authority to preach and cast out demons while leaving them with firm instructions on what to take for the journey (Luke 10).

We know that in his childhood Jesus had aunts and uncles he traveled with to and from Jerusalem (Luke 2). He worked in the family business with Joseph and a salty assortment of tradesmen and day laborers. It should be telling that, after his resurrection, Jesus had some five hundred people gathered around him when he ascended (1 Corinthians 15:3–9). Jesus lived among and shared life within a tight-knit community. Eugene H. Peterson, translating John's gospel, put it this way: "The Word became flesh and blood, and *moved into the neighborhood*" (John 1:14 THE MESSAGE, emphasis added).

Having read so much about the ancient religions and myths written about the gods, it boggles my mind that Christianity so unashamedly articulates the story of Jesus as the God of the common people. He is the God of the

Monday morning breakfast diner, chatting it up with the old, retired curmudgeons. He is the God of the city square, walking the streets, talking with vendors, and playing with the preschool-aged children whose mothers just need a nap (Matthew 19:14). He is the God who convenes the community around the campfire for late nights filled with good food, wild stories, and deep laughter.

Most of the gods of Greek mythology either don't *need* companionship or don't *have time* for it. Or maybe we should say that they aren't set up for it. Friendship would be incompatible for their brand of deity. The ancient gods don't mix with mere mortals. But the first thing that happens to God the Son is to be born into a complex and perplexing family dynamic. Jesus grew up in a home that would have been the talk of the town. Locals undoubtedly whispered about Mary and Joseph and the unexpected pregnancy. *God dwells right there*, honoring friendship and familial bonds.

God the Son went to weekly synagogue services and to the local house of worship with extended relatives and eccentric characters within the community. God the Son *had friends* and loved them so fully that he wept when they died (Lazarus in John 11:35), and he loved the disciples so much that before he died, he gathered them all around a table to share a meal. This ministry of friendship that Jesus made known to the world *came from somewhere*.

We have accounts of him feeding the multitudes and sitting down on a grassy hillside to teach the crowds. He was so wildly compassionate and impossibly patient with them. He took time with ailing widows and bereaved fathers. He giddily let the little children come to him and kissed them on their foreheads with the affirmation of heaven. Jesus was a divine magnet for all the world's disaffected, for all the ones suffering and "oppressed of the devil" (Acts 10:38 KJV).

Here's a little glimpse of a day in the life of Jesus:

> That evening after sunset the people brought to Jesus *all the sick and demon-possessed*. The *whole town* gathered at the door, and Jesus healed many who had various diseases. He also drove out many demons. (Mark 1:32–34, emphasis added)

It took me a while to notice a very important textual detail: all the sick and demon-possessed were brought to Jesus "after sunset" (v. 32). Did people wait for it to get dark because that was when they felt safe enough to bring them out of hiding? Probably. And still, Jesus gladly received them. He'd already had a full day of conversation and prayer, of teaching and reaching out to the beleaguered. Evening is supposed to be when you retire and rest. But Jesus was so special that he was just getting started when everyone else was winding down! He sent them home with happy hearts, quiet minds, and full bellies. Their cups were overflowing, but Jesus was now surely depleted.

After long stretches of being with people, Jesus regularly disbanded the large crowds and even snuck away from his friends. He disappeared. Mark the evangelist put it this way:

> Very early in the morning, while it was still dark, Jesus got up, left the house and went off to a solitary place, where he prayed. (1:35)

You know Jesus had his go-to spots. The little shoreline cove tucked away along the coast of Capernaum where the *lap*, *lap*, *lap* of the water slowly washed away the chaos of the day, dragging it into the depths and leaving Jesus refreshed. You know he snuck away to the fragrant grove of olive trees with that lush lawn that promised the best naps. Yes, he is the Son of God, but he was also the son of Mary, which means he got tired like you and me. And the Son needed regular solitude to get his soul back.

But what did he *do* when he disappeared? The Gospels tell us these were times of prayer. And what is prayer anyway? It is surely one of the most confused and confusing categories in the life of faith. So I'll burn down at least a couple of straw-man approaches to prayer.

Prayer is not an executive meeting that we lead where we share our daily agenda and create a punch list for the counsel of heaven to start working on. Prayer is not about clocking in so the boss upstairs knows we showed up to work and did our duty for the day. Prayer is primarily *communion*. Communion *with God*. And Jesus, when he disappeared, was fleeing the noise, the swirl, the chaos, and entering into a concentrated and unbroken communion. To pray rightly, then, sometimes requires that you say nothing. Prayer is *being there*, with God. Listening, breathing, centering down, hearing him pronounce your name in *that voice*, getting your soul restored and the ill-fitting yoke of the world off your neck.

It is important, though, for us to remember *who* Jesus was communing with. He was communing with *his Father*. And communion at its essence is *friendship*. Jesus drove the crowds away because he longed for an undistracted audience with his Father. He wanted to talk. He wanted to listen. He wanted to share his heart and maybe even his fears about Calvary and the cross that was crashing down on him. Communion also includes celebration. *My Father, did you see their faces? Can you believe how happy they were? Did you see the wonder wash over them when those five loaves fed all fifteen thousand of them?*

Jesus said, "The Son can do nothing of his own accord, but only what he *sees* the Father doing" (John 5:19 ESV, emphasis added), which means that a true life of prayer is about *gazing*. It means that prayer finds its perfected form when daughters and sons stop and stare at the glorious grace to be found in the Father's eyes. So prayer is communion, and communion arises from friendship. And—now hear this startling claim from Christian theology—God *is* friendship. I did not say, "God is friendly," though I guess we might easily affirm that too. But stopping at "God is friendly" is too precious; it falls far short of the forceful claim that God *exists as friendship.*

Yes, I said, "God *is* friendship." How can I say that? And what might the implications of such a statement be?

For a couple of thousand years, the church has insisted on the scintillating specificity of God as Trinity—Father, Son, and Holy Spirit. We are told that God is not some amorphous blob of divinity, emanating good vibes and positive energy from somewhere out there in the ether. God is not a static oneness of solitary confinement. God *is* the holy Trinity, the holy tri-unity. God's oneness is seen in God's *three*-ness, and his wholeness is expressed in communion.

For God is love, and love cannot be love without another to receive and reciprocate it.

For a couple of thousand years, the church has been praying "in the name of the Father and of the Son and of the Holy Spirit" (Matthew 28:19). And two thousand years ago, before he ascended and returned to dwell in the unbounded blessedness of his Father's gaze, Jesus commanded his disciples—and by extension us—to make disciples. But his instructions went further. When they had become disciples, they were to be baptized into the "name of the Father and of the Son and of the Holy Spirit."

Why does it matter that God is properly understood as Trinity? It matters because God as Trinity means that God, in his very essence, is a divine communion of unmitigated love. Philosopher and Christian writer Dallas Willard said that God as Trinity means that God is a constant ecstatic celebration.[2] It means that friendship is the substructure at the subterranean core of the Godhead. It means that friendship is the first existential reality, the first institution. Friendship is *pre*primordial. God the Father didn't say "This is my Son, whom I love" for the first time at Jesus's baptism (Matthew 3:17). God the Father has been saying it from all eternity past, long before he ever said, "Let there be light!" Just like the birth of a child can be the natural consequence of a couple caught up in holy communion, the created order—the entire world—is the natural consequence of the love of the Godhead. Love creates.

And if, as the writer of Hebrews said, "Jesus Christ is the same yesterday and today and forever" (13:8), then it must mean that he didn't say, "Father, into your hands I commit my spirit" (Luke 23:46), for the first time when he was suffocating to death on the cross. A theology of the Trinity helps us understand that the Son has been saying that to his Father from eternity past and will be saying it world without end.

We could say it like this: God loves God. Which is another way of saying the Father is eternally crazy about his Son, and the Son is forever enamored of his Father. And the love and mutuality and friendship and unbroken blessedness of holy communion they share *is* the Holy Spirit. Yes, the Holy Spirit is the bond of love that "proceeds from the Father and the Son" into all the world.[3] The Holy Spirit shoots out into all the world like a lasso of divine love, wrapping us up and pulling us deeper into friendship with the triune God and friendship with one another.

And if it's true that God is Trinity, it must also mean that we live in a befriended world, a world where friendship is not only *possible* but where friendship is *natural*. The whole created cosmos—of which the earth is an infinitesimally small part—is enfolded within and animated by friendship.

No, God is not just friendly. God *is* friendship. And if we are made in his image (Genesis 1:26–28), then it follows that a longing for friendship must certainly be encoded into us. In short, when we live in holy friendship—the giving and receiving, the kindness and compassion, the pouring out of oneself to and for another—we are becoming more like God.

Trinitarian theology creates a Christian social ethic. Theology has implications. We first learn that we are made *from* love, which means we are made *for* love. Friendship is the great gift that Christian theology introduces to the world. For "it is not good that [mankind] should be alone" (Genesis 2:18 ESV).

The Three Threats of Friendship

Friendship is your heart becoming fond of someone else, your heart beginning to find its home with another person, your relational roots beginning to take. And friendship aids fixity in place. We long to stay somewhere when relationships are rich. So if friendship is God's gift to us, and if friendship aides our stability in place, you can bet it will be threatened by the Enemy. I believe there are three primary threats that keep us from receiving the gift of friendship.

The first is *our blatant individualism*. All too often we buy into the narrative of the cutthroat corporate ladder climbers. It's a dog-eat-dog world out there, and if we're going to make it, it'll be because we take it from our fiercest competitors. This is the darkest and most deranged form of individualism, for sure, but there are subtler forms too. Many of us have simply learned to live alone. We have grown accustomed to keeping our heads down and burying ourselves in our work. A global pandemic that sent us all into lockdown didn't help either. Speaking to strangers seems to be a dying art form. Even good churchgoers can be high-functioning individualists, sneaking in the back during worship to hear an inspiring talk for their own spiritual development and then bolting before the benediction is over. These are the people who don't need to—or don't *want* to—ask for help.

The second threat that stands in the way of our receiving

the gift of friendship is *our dizzying busyness*. We *want* to have deep friendships, but we don't *have time* for friends. Whether you're in the cities or in the suburbs, time is constrained, the bottleneck is clogged by our crazy calendars. Commuters spend precious hours in cars, hours that we would love to devote to our favorite people. Single professionals often find themselves working fifty to sixty hours a week, and by the time they are free to get together, they often find themselves too tired. Parents are taxiing the kids to soccer or to piano or to dance or to gymnastics or to school productions, and if a night magically opens up, they *might* be able to get them to youth group at the church. Give that calendar a once-over and tell me where the time is going to get carved out for meaningful friendships.

The third threat to friendship is *our pathological avoidance of conflict*. I spoke about this in chapter 5 ("Honoring Your Relationships: People Are the Great Purifiers"), so I won't belabor the point. But if you're going to have friends, at some point the honeymoon phase will be over. Something will happen that causes an offense, and in the moment of offense, it feels easier to run. But if we are going to have friends over the long haul, we are going to have to overcome the quick fix of conflict avoidance and do the hard work of making things right.

Fighting for Friendship

So if friendship is what God is made of, and if friendship is his great gift to us, then how do we fight to preserve it?

Lifelong friendship is formed by regular routines. Which is to say that friendship has to be planned for and calendared. I remember being young and thinking that anything true and fun had to be spontaneous. But now that I am older and a little bit wiser, I say that if it's worth anything to you, it's worth *planning for.*

I can't tell you how many times I have been at a Christmas party with friends I see once or twice a year and thought, *Goodness, these are such great people and I love them to death. I just wish I could see them!* A meme went around a couple of years ago that would be funny if it weren't so true: "Adult friendship is two people saying, 'I haven't seen you in forever; we should really hang out more' over and over again until one of them dies."

There are a thousand ways to build routines that become rich relationship, but the work of planning must be done. For some it'll be a monthly dinner with a few friends or a couple of young families. For others it'll be taking summer camping trips together. I know families that take a yearly vacation together and others that swap childcare on date nights. I know single folks who do weekly meal groups together and tired young moms who do book groups with friends. I do two all-day retreats every year with a handful of friends I've known for two decades. They are some of the best memories I have.

Yes, there are a thousand ways to work toward deepening friendship. You can get out your calendar and build a meaningful year however you want. But in a world starved of friendship, please just do it. The world was born from friendship. And you need it more than you know.

CHAPTER 11

STABILITY IN CHURCH

If you wish to keep peace and live in harmony
with others, you must learn to abdicate your
will in many things. *It is no small matter to live
in a monastery or a congregation and abide there
without complaint and persevere faithfully until
death.* Blessed is he who has lived well the
monastic life and has brought it to a happy end.

—*Thomas à Kempis, emphasis added*

ONE OF THE GREATEST WAYS TO ESTABLISH stability in your life is to find a local church and stay there as long as you can. But let me warn you up front that it will be hard to do! In the previous chapter, I highlighted how we often run when relational conflict arises. This happens in churches too.

Over nearly two decades as a pastor, I have talked with plenty of people who were leaving our church. I'm not talking about the people who were moving out of town because of a job transfer or a new military assignment. I'm not talking about the people who of necessity were moving cross-country to care for aging parents who were all alone. I'm talking about people who were just changing churches. I know people who have lived in Colorado Springs for fifteen years and are in their fifth church. Now, let me say this again as clearly as I can: I'm not romanticizing stability and pretending that we can all stay in the same place forever. I realize things shift and there are times for change. I realize there are unhealthy environments that, when discovered, need to be avoided.

Still, so many of the departures I have witnessed through the years feel like an adolescent case of conflict avoidance. Instead of doing the soul-searching work of conversation and confrontation and conflict resolution that can lead to forgiveness, many people just disappear. And so they move to the next place and start completely over, dragging their hurts and offenses with them. As the fifteenth-century monk Thomas à Kempis observed, "Wherever you go, there you are!"[1] They don't realize they are only prolonging their relational rootlessness.

Or maybe we leave because our consumer culture has developed all the wrong appetites in us and trained us to look for the best customer experience in town. As a culture, we have been discipled by phrases like "The customer is always right," so people often walk into a church as *potential* congregants having already been shaped by a market mindset. We are looking for a customized church experience that's tailor-made to meet *our needs*, one that fits *our family* just right.

And sometimes people leave because they're simply bored. They need a new adventure. They've been walking into this same old sanctuary that's needed a new paint job for seven years. They've been listening to this same old preacher and that same old worship team. I've actually heard people say things like this:

- "Yeah, yeah. I've got it. When are we going to do something *new* around here?"
- "These people are too unsophisticated for the path I'm on."
- "Sure, they got me to where I am, but they can't take me to where I'm going."

The church is not the place to get all your felt needs met. Jesus didn't intend the church to be your spiritual clearinghouse of inspiration and self-fulfillment. The church is not like the posh Delta Sky Club lounge at the airport, feeding your spiritual hunger and giving you a place to put your feet up before another long week. The church is the crucible that makes us disciples, the furnace that burns away selfishness and self-preference and every notion of a life of self-fulfillment and forges a purity of faith that is an affront to a world intoxicated with *the self.* I should add: the church is the crucible that makes us disciples *if we will let it.* And sometimes the only way we can let it make us disciples is to stay when we want to bolt.

> The church is the crucible that makes us disciples.

Or maybe I should say it this way: if you're not being inconvenienced regularly in church, you're probably doing it wrong. I'm thinking about the inconvenience of putting on a reflective vest and wielding an orange flashlight to help park cars at the Christmas Eve services when twice-a-year parishioners *and* full-blooded pagans are flooding the parking lot. I'm thinking about the inconvenience of volunteering to pull off the junior high retreat with a group of other sleep-deprived parents. I'm thinking about the inconvenience of gathering regularly with a small group of folks to pray, even when those people vote differently than you and earn in a different tax bracket from you. I'm thinking about the inconvenience of tithing every month when that same money could easily fund a weekend place for your family to enjoy in the mountains.

As I study the life of Jesus, I see a life regularly riddled with inconveniences, littered with interruptions, caught up in the nagging circumstances of ordinary people. He had a magnetic force that drew in wailing widows and beleaguered businessmen, frantic parents, angry spiritual leaders, and power-hungry politicians. Jesus couldn't even go to a wedding as an anonymous spectator. The wedding coordinator saw a need, freaked out, and ran over to him. The Lord's first miracle was having to come up with something for everyone to drink. Yes, if inconvenience isn't right there at the top of your church experience, you're probably doing it wrong. But I can also tell you that by committing to and persevering through the inconveniences you will gain the greatest treasures. The treasure of deep relationships. The holy satisfaction of self-emptying love. The purity that emerges through the furnace of fidelity. The unquantifiable wealth of a life steeped in stability in place.

Maybe Jesus knows that inconvenience is the gift we didn't know we needed. Which is why, in the fifteenth century, Thomas à Kempis was able to say, "It is no small matter to live in a monastery or a congregation and abide there *without complaint* and persevere faithfully *until death.*" He knew where the treasure could be found. And so he encouraged us to try to die where we are.

When Technology Outpaces Our Theology

There is still another subtle seduction standing in the way of our commitment to a church. We say things like "I *am* the church" while many of us have no local church. If we *do* attend a church, many of us change churches like we change gyms—whenever the other place down the street has nicer facilities, newer equipment, or better childcare. Still, many of us are leaving the church wholesale while imagining we are in step with Jesus. What I see all too regularly is an inordinate number of people who have no relational rootage, no weekly routines of gathering together with the saints.

Worship, which was always a *communal* act in ancient Israel's history, has now been privatized and commoditized. We have our podcasts and YouTube channels. We have our favorite internet pastors—a phrase that would surely make the apostle Paul turn over in his grave—and watch from the comfort of our couches curled up in our bathrobes with our favorite coffee mug in hand. Indeed, we have discovered we can get our sermons and songs without having to trifle with other saints and sinners. Of course, during COVID-19 we all rejoiced that we could do these things. It was a necessity, a temporary saving grace. But we must be careful not to let our *technology* outpace our *theology*. There is a sad irony: God who in Jesus became incarnate now has a people being tempted to live lives of *dis*incarnation.

In times like this, we would do well to remember that such an experiment is possible only in the developed world. I was in the Middle East earlier this year, working with Syrian and Iraqi refugees. The year before I went to a secure location and met with twelve underground Iranian pastors who were living their lives ready to die, living knowing that the baptismal waters in which they are burying people into Christ could easily run red with blood at any moment by the hand of an evil regime. For the people of the developing world, *gathering with* and being *insinuated into* a local church is a must and often means the difference between life and death, between eating and going without. They don't have the option of living a churchless, privatized spirituality. And while most of them own very little, they have a richness of spirit and vitality of community that we in the West have lost and desperately need to regain. They know a deep truth that we in our information age cannot Google search our way into.

Buy Your Burial Plots

Just so everyone knows the playing field is level, I should say that it isn't just *parishioners* who struggle with staying in a church. *Pastors* do too. It was refreshing to hear Pastor Bob Beckett of the Dwelling Place in Hemet, California, name the allure that was threatening to draw him away from the church he was serving.

Bob came out of his seminary training ready to *change the world*, ready to do *something that mattered*. But he also had loans to pay off, so an entry-level job in Hemet would have to do. Hemet, an old western cattle-ranching town in the San Jacinto Valley, wasn't exactly situated at the crossroads of culture and commerce. *We all have to start somewhere*, he thought. For Bob, the Dwelling Place was always going to be a stepping-stone on his vocational path. He thought he would serve these people for a couple of years until he could find a more significant place. I say this with a great sense of irony. Imagine a parent deciding to serve their first child for a few years until a more significant child came along! There are no insignificant churches just as there are no insignificant children. But Bob was going to have to learn this lesson over time.

For years he experienced a deep sense of ineffectiveness in his work. Folks were staying away from his church by the thousands. And people at his church were at one another's throats; he couldn't seem to broker peace with any of them. The ministry of reconciliation the apostle Paul commended was elusive to Bob. The seeds of gospel proclamation that Bob had been planting didn't seem to be coming up in a rich harvest of salvation. *What is going on here?* he thought. Bob read Jesus's words in the Gospels where he gave his disciples authority to preach and teach, to gather all the scattered and sinful, to cast out unclean spirits and heal the sick (Matthew 10:1; Mark 3:14–15). But Bob felt handcuffed. He knew something was wrong.

Charles Kraft, a longtime theologian at Fuller Theological Seminary, has for decades been interested in learning what gives pastors spiritual authority to do their work in a parish or a defined geographical place. He sat down with Bob for an interview and then drafted a summary of Bob's *root-lessness*, which he believed was the cause of those years of *fruitlessness* in Hemet:

> The turning point came when [Bob] heard the Lord asking him, *What is your commitment to Hemet?* This stunned Bob. He thought, *What a question! Who in his right mind commits himself to a place like Hemet?* But he realized, "I could never begin to bring deliverance of any real and lasting significance to my own area if

I was living here with my emotional and spiritual bags packed, always waiting for the day when the Lord would call me to a larger community with greater influence and significance."[2]

It's not just small-town pastors who struggle with this. I interviewed Louie Giglio a couple of years ago with some friends. Giglio is the founder of the Passion movement, which has gathered millions of college students and twentysomethings since 1997. He has traveled extensively and published prolifically. In our conversation, he talked about his decades of living on the move, living from conference to conference.

When I was younger, I thought the way you make the biggest impact on the world is you go to the most places you can and speak to the most people you can speak to. At forty I had a wakeup moment where I realized that you make the greatest impact by *staying in the same place for the longest amount of time* to see the reproductive power of the gospel at work in the generational cycles that come.[3]

After living on airplanes, after eating his way through greenrooms, after staying in a thousand different hotel rooms, Giglio said, "I wanted to root somewhere." So he and his bride, Shelley, repositioned their energy and planted Passion City Church in Atlanta. He said, "It's been the hardest thing we've ever done, and the greatest time we've ever had."[4]

Surprisingly, even Billy Graham, America's most

well-known evangelist of the twentieth century, had regrets about his rootlessness in place. Toward the end of his long life, he said,

> Although I have much to be grateful for as I look back over my life, I also have many regrets. I have failed many times, and I would do many things differently. For one thing, I would speak less and study more, and I would spend more time with my family.
>
> When I look back over the schedule I kept thirty or forty years ago, I am staggered by all the things we did and the engagements we kept. Sometimes we flitted from one part of the country to another, even from one continent to another, in the course of only a few days. Were all those engagements necessary? Was I as discerning as I might have been about which ones to take and which to turn down? I doubt it. Every day I was absent from my family is gone forever. Although much of that travel was necessary, some of it was not.[5]

After discovering the importance of place, Pastor Bob Beckett of Hemet and his bride unpacked their bags and did the most shocking thing: they went to the local cemetery and bought two burial plots. They decided they would give their lives to *those people* in *that place*—and they would try to die there. The result was almost instantaneous. Peace came within the church. Of course, there were the ongoing, garden-variety nagging concerns that arise in any church, but people were now being saved and baptized and discipled afresh. Joy was springing up. Bob and his bride were falling in love with the quirks and the character and even the unsavory people of Hemet. Something had shifted in the unseen realm that could now be seen everywhere they looked.

Kraft summarized it this way:

> There is a direct relationship between the commitment of a pastor (or any leader) and the authority he or she wields in the spirit world. Pastors who are committed to something other than their churches are vulnerable to enemy influence. Though serving the church, their primary commitment may really be to their own advancement or something else (such as money, prestige or an easy life). We cannot expect the spirit world to take them seriously when they assert their authority over the church and the people . . . they purport to serve.[6]

So, pastors, do your best to unpack your bags. Walk to a local cemetery. Buy your burial plots. Pick a place, put down roots, and see what kind of fruit comes from your pursuit of stability.

Finding Home Near the Big City

It is a noisy night in New York City. Taxi drivers are honking their horns and cutting in front of the uninitiated tourists who are clogging the streets with their slow-moving rental cars. Street performers from every nation under heaven are holding court, singing and dancing and hawking cheap trinkets and doing card tricks under the bright lights. A few bankers are eating surf and turf at the Chart House on the Hudson River, closing a deal that's been in the works for months now. This is the restaurant for celebrations because of its panoramic views of the city's skyline.

But in the shadow of this place, one of the most transient cities in the world, you can find some saints who can teach you a lot about cultivating stability in church. If you're on the Hudson River, all you have to do is shuffle over a couple of suburbs to the north to Bergen County, to the place known as Wyckoff, New Jersey.

Once you get there, walk into Bethany Church on a Sunday morning or a Wednesday night and ask to be introduced to Jack and Rose Egan. They have been worshipping at Bethany every week for forty-one years. The Egans have worked hard to build a successful business in New York City, but they've worked even harder to help their three sons grow up in the company of an extended family of faith. People like the Tates, the Browns, the Maffeis, the Imperials, the Vallones, and the Jameses. Bethany Church is the place the Egans dedicated and baptized their sons.

Countless times over forty-one years, when someone at Bethany Church came upon hard times, Jack and Rose ran to the front of the line, opening their hearts and their checkbooks, showing hospitality and sharing in the burden until the burden was lifted. During forty-one years in the same church, they've celebrated as their friends' children married and they've wept as their friends' parents were buried. Over forty-one years they've set up chairs and led small groups and volunteered on youth retreats and sent their kids on global missions. They've gone into hospitals to pray and into living rooms to counsel fractured families. They've served as elders and given their all for the preservation of the saints gathered at Bethany Church. And, of course, along the way, they've given financially. They've given forty-one years of tithes and offerings as just one more sign of their commitment to *that place* and *those people*.

I had dinner recently with Jack and Rose. Because I admire them so deeply, I asked them about the challenges and the unique joys of staying in one place for over four decades. Sure, there were challenges and annoyances and difficult people along the way. But then Rose said, "But where else are we going to go? These are our people!"

At the end of our dinner, I thanked them for their fidelity, their stability, their dogged determination to live faithfully among the saints at Bethany Church in Wyckoff. As a pastor who has watched so many people casually come and go over the years, I wanted them to know there are people like me drawing strength from their commitment. I thanked them for praying, for teaching, for loving, and for giving financially for forty-one years. Jack, one of the funniest people I know, cracked a tithing joke, and the room erupted with laughter. Then he said something that stopped me in my tracks: "If Rosie and I hadn't tithed all these years, we would have a lot more money. But we wouldn't be as *rich*."

Yes, Jack and Rose have given their money, but they haven't *just* given their money. That would have been too cheap of an exchange. They've given the whole of their lives, their hearts, and the hospitality of their home. To the same people. For forty-one years. And you should too. For the one who does so is truly rich indeed.

True riches, says the sage Jack Egan, are not found in bottom lines and bank accounts. True riches are found when people commit their lives to one another, when people do the hard work of staying when it would be easier to run. True riches are found when your children have a church full of extended aunts and uncles in the faith.

So stop running. Like Thomas Merton and Rose and Jack Egan, see if you can stay with the same saints for a few decades. Rediscover the power of place. And then try to die there. Because there are compounding riches that can only be found on the other side of your fidelity in place.

> True riches are found when people commit their lives to one another, when people do the hard work of staying when it would be easier to run.

CHAPTER 12

STABILITY IN COMMUNITY

Cities have the capability of providing
something for everybody, only because, and
only when, they are created by everybody.
—*Jane Jacobs*

OUR PRACTICES OF STABILITY HAVE MOVED increasingly outward in graduating concentric circles. The first practice we discussed roots us in our *homes*, our physical residences, and calls us to make a home as an act of creation. From there we move outward to practice stability with our *families*, then our *friends*, and then our *church*. The final practice of stability we'll address is stability in our *communities*. The towns, cities, suburbs, and streets where we live. We want to ask in this chapter what it looks like to contribute to the flourishing of the place where we all share our common life together.

Reading church history can help us here. Because when you read church history, the fact becomes inescapably clear: the saints are always from *somewhere*. Think about it. We've got Perpetua *of* Carthage, Augustine *of* Hippo, Hildegard *of* Bingen, and Francis *of* Assisi. Eugene H. Peterson once quipped, "Geography is as important in the Christian way as Christology."[1] I'm always struck by how every significant saintly contribution was at first so unspectacularly *local*. We peer back into history and romanticize their contributions as having had some sort of universal impact, but the saints, instead of trying to change the world, have always started by trying to change their neighborhoods.

Teresa *of* Calcutta, the Albanian-born woman of slight frame—the woman who later became a global icon and the weathered face of the struggle against poverty—never set out to become an icon. She simply stepped out of the safety of the convent's walls and wandered into the surrounding slum.

> The saints, instead of trying to change the world, have always started by trying to change their neighborhoods.

It was in the midst of the Bengal famine of 1943 that her life was arrested and her heart was broken for the poor. The rest is history. The small woman lived a big life. We tend to think of the hundreds of thousands of people who were marked by her sacrifice, but it all started when she looked one very sick person in the eyes. She supposedly said, "Not all of us can do great things. But we can all do small things with great love."

Yes, if you want to become a saint, you have to be willing to submit to the smallest of all prepositions: *of*. Indeed, before the eternal Word stretched out his arms on the cross to take on the weight of sin and death, he took on a preposition: Jesus *of* Nazareth. Even Jesus didn't try to live outside of the community that was right in front of him. Apparently, the way you make a big difference is by giving yourself over to the concerns and the constraints of a small place.

Two Guiding Metaphors

So how do we think about our work and witness in the places we live? We need guiding images and metaphors to hold on to that can help us live well in our particular places.

The first metaphor: imagine the place in which you live as a *garden* and you as the *gardener*. Going back to the beginning of this book—indeed, to the beginning of *creation*—imagine yourself as being turned loose by God in your own Edenic garden. There will be areas around you in which life is breaking out. Certain neighbors will be living in a neighborly fashion, cooperating and creating an atmosphere that leads to flourishing. Their home will be like a fruitful row in your garden. Being a good gardener, you pay attention. You notice sections of the garden that are abounding with fertility. So the first thing you do is notice it and name it. These people may not even be aware of what they're doing, but the very act of you noticing it and naming it creates a value system. It reinforces the right kinds of behavior and demonstrates to the people around the garden that this place, the place they all share in common, will operate on a culture of celebration. A good gardener tends and waters what is working. Shine light on the beauty of a place and help others recognize it as beautiful.

If you have school-aged children, maybe you can treat the school they attend as your own little garden. Serve the teachers, help lead a reading group in one of the classes, uproot anything that is an obvious hindrance, anything that feels like a gnarly weed. If you notice your school is short on supplies because of budget cuts, help rally people to raise the funds. Plant good seeds. Tend the fragile students. Be a light that catalyzes their growth. Everywhere you are can be thought of as a garden, with you as the gardener.

Maybe you sense a call to civic engagement. Go for it. We need as many folks as we can get who are ready to heed

Jeremiah's words, folks who are ready to seek the peace and prosperity of their local places. Maybe you'll work to reclaim a public park or a city playground in a long-neglected neighborhood. Maybe the Lord will break your heart for the homeless and you'll spend your strength working toward the creation of affordable multiunit housing. The garden is big. The possibilities are everywhere. Now's the time for you to practice that skilled mastery you've been working on all these years.

The second metaphor: imagine the people situated around you as a *congregation* and you as their *pastor*. There will be children running around your street who need someone to notice them. Learn their names. Many of them will live in homes filled with strife and instability. Many of them will not have food in their pantries. A significant part of your pastoral duties will be making cookies for these children and having Popsicles in your freezer for hot summer afternoons. Let them know that your lawn is *their* lawn and your driveway is *their* driveway. If you live this way, you will re-enchant the neighborhood. Relationships will develop. Trust will rise. If you live this way, they will instinctively know where they'll find kindness and lots of candy on Halloween. And if you live this way, expect to receive lots of graduation announcements and wedding invitations a couple of decades from now.

All the neighborhood children you cared for will grow up feeling the strength of their increased social capital. They will know they have *you* in their corner. They will sense the safety of your presence, and their worlds will be enlarged because of it. When you are old, they will remember you and visit you when they return home for Thanksgiving and Christmas. And when you enter your eternal rest, they will cry at your funeral and honor your memory as they live the life of neighborliness you taught them.

On your street there will likely be an elderly woman who lives alone and needs to be visited and cared for and listened to. In the years to come, she may need you to drive her to a medical appointment. Let her know in advance that when that time comes, she doesn't need to look any further for help. *You* would be happy to be her chauffeur. Take another neighbor with you when you visit her so the web of relationships can be broadened and the community can function more fully as a family unit. Remember, you are the pastor of your street, and your neighbors are your parishioners.

What I have found is that often there is a direct correlation between one's service to a community and one's stability within it. To the degree that you *build others up* in your local place is the degree that your *roots go down*. To the degree that you create stability for others is the degree to which you will experience stability yourself. For as the prophet Isaiah said,

> If you spend yourselves in behalf of the hungry
>> and satisfy the needs of the oppressed,
> then your light will rise in the darkness,
>> and your night will become like the noonday.
> The LORD will guide you always;
>> he will satisfy your needs in a sun-scorched land
>> and will strengthen your frame.
> You will be like a well-watered garden,

like a spring whose waters never fail.
Your people will rebuild the ancient ruins
and will raise up the age-old foundations;
you will be called Repairer of Broken Walls,
Restorer of Streets with Dwellings. (58:10–12)

CHAPTER 13

A SACRED STAY

No race can prosper until it learns there is as
much dignity in tilling a field as in writing a poem.
—*Booker T. Washington*

I COME FROM A LONG LINE OF AGRARIANS, salt-of-the-earth farmers and ranchers, and lovers of the land who lived in small towns across Washington and northern Idaho. The patches of skin that for decades were exposed to the scorching sun and howling wind—the forearms and hands, the ears, the back of the neck—were permanently transfigured, a collage of various colorations arranged on one body. There's a reason they call it a farmer's tan.

As a family, we treasure the fifty years' worth of daily journal entries that were scribed by my great-great-grandmother Lula Wilson and her daughter-in-law, my great-grandmother, Lucille Kemp Wilson. Lula and Lucille were the most recent matriarchs in my line. These journals give a glimpse into the life of a family living on a rural farm. You can thumb your way through Lula's journal and see the textures of a rural community just as the darkness of the Great Depression was descending across the land. Here are a few of those entries from 1930:

> **June 30:** 16 loads of hay hauled in today. Burl [her son], Mick, Elmer and a stranger worked. Lucille and all the children are here. White sow bred today.

> **September 6:** Little yellow calf born.

September 22: Canned 6 quarts of beans, 6 quarts of corn. Fried 2 chickens for dinner. Finished digging potatoes, 10 sacks.

December 25: A beautiful morn—Burl called to wish all a merry Christmas—a wonderful Xmas, grand dinner, the table looked beautiful, the dinner was swell.

Lula was an amputee, having lost a leg to diabetes. Can you imagine the quality of the health care along the back-country roads of small-town Washington? Health care was virtually nonexistent, but somehow Lula made it. Their existence was spare and spartan, and they prayed that famous line from the Lord's prayer literally: "Give us this day our daily bread" (Matthew 6:11 ESV). On August 17, 1901, Lula had a son who would much later become my great-grandfather. His name was George Burl Wilson. Young George grew tall, and at least to his father's eyes, his gangly, narrow legs looked like thin boards, like skinny slats of wood. So he was nicknamed Slats.

But my agrarian ancestors were also fantastic musicians. The banjo was their instrument of choice, the rhythmic and melodic backbone of the family band, and whenever they would gather in the living room or around a bonfire, everyone sang their part—soprano, alto, tenor, bass. Great-grandpa Slats demonstrated a knack for the banjo and quickly became a rising star in the region. In his early twenties he started playing professionally, joining the Mann Brothers Orchestra.

This was America's era of vaudevillian music, of the

dance halls and concert saloons, and the seven young men toured the country, playing the Pantages Theater Circuit, a robust franchise with eighty-four theaters across the country. One show was at the sold-out Algeria Amphitheater in Helena, Montana, which boasted 2,608 seats! At that time the largest concert hall in the nation was the Hippodrome Theatre in New York City, which had 4,588 seats. The Mann Brothers Orchestra played a stretch of weekly shows in Lewiston, Idaho, that had more than 5,000 people dancing on the lawn every Friday night. These guys were small-town boys from Idaho and Washington, and they were taking the nation by storm. Everywhere they played they wore expensive tailored tuxedos, quite a departure from the bib overalls and boots they grew up wearing on their family farms.

But one night in Kansas City, and out of nowhere, my great-grandpa Slats walked off the stage and quit the band. An invisible fault line had shifted in the economy, and the nation was in tremors. Deep fissures were splitting open. They were now seeing the bottom of the Great Depression. Several of Slats's musician friends were having to stand in soup lines from town to town to find a meal. So he quit, telling his bandmates he'd never be seen standing in a soup line, waiting for a meal. To casual observers, this may sound like pride. But knowing my family heritage as I do, I actually think it was the response of a man who felt duty bound to serve his nation in a moment of national crisis. Instead of asking for bread, he'd go home and grow wheat that would help feed his country. He grew up on the land and knew how to nurture it into a luxuriant yield. He knew that the nation would need farmers to carry her through these years, so he quit the band, got on the first train heading west from Kansas City, and went back home.

During Slats's first year back on the farm, he regularly wore his expensive tuxedo as he plowed the fields. Can you imagine a man riding behind his draft horses plowing a field in a tuxedo? The Pulitzer Prize–winning writer Marilynne Robinson remembered her grandfather working his garden in his best suits too.[1] "They were just too nice to throw away," said Great-grandpa Slats.

Slats may have thought he was just being frugal, but I think there is a deeper meaning for those who care to pay attention. We wear tuxedos when we know we're involved with the sacred. We wear tuxedos when we want to hallow a moment. We wear tuxedos as a threaded signal that we recognize we've been tangled up in the eternal. By wearing his tuxedo to work on the farm, I think Slats was onto something. The land is a place to hallow the Name, a beautiful sacrament to be received and enjoyed.

On his first day back on the farm, I imagine my great-grandpa Slats getting up early and getting ready for the day. He was back to his place of birth, back to the backbreaking work on the land. There would be no adoring fans to cheer him. There would be no fancy lighting or boisterous introductions. There would be no elevated stage and no one dancing just below it. Just a man, his family land, and a tuxedo.

At the burning bush, Moses was told to take off his sandals, "for the place where you are standing is holy ground" (Exodus 3:5). On that first day, I can imagine Slats hearing something like: *Put on your tuxedo. For the place where you are standing is holy ground.*

And the place you are standing is holy as well. My prayer is that this book will serve as a fresh call to consecrate the ground underneath your feet. I pray that you begin to see yourself as Saint _____ of _____. Insert your name and your place in those blanks. And let it always be a reminder of the power of place.

AFTERWORD

When You Can't Stay

How to Honor Stability When You Have to Live on the Move

Seek the peace and prosperity of the city to which
I have carried you into exile. Pray to the LORD for
it, because if it prospers, you too will prosper.

—*Jeremiah 29:7*

AFTER READING A BOOK TITLED *THE POWER OF Place*, a book that calls us to take the vow of stability as best we can, it would be easy to romanticize living in one place for the rest of your life. But the reality is that life rarely works out so neatly.

There are plenty of people who would *love* to stay in one place for a long time and put down roots, but they simply aren't able to. There are military families who are required to move to a new assignment every few years. There are people who live at the mercy of economic migration patterns that keep them shifting from region to region, following where work leads them. There are family responsibilities that arise unexpectedly that result in a move: the death of a loved one, the loss or change of a job, an aging parent who now needs daily care and companionship, a grandchild born with special needs who will require extra help. There are moments in all our lives when our romantic notions of being able to call our own shots are quickly dashed against the jagged rocks of real life.

Thankfully, the ancient witness of Scripture knows what to do with the dynamism of real life. The biblical writers aren't shocked about *anything*, even an unexpected and unsettling and heartbreaking move. Have you ever thought about the fact that one of the predominant themes of the Old Testament is the theme of *exile*? Adam and Eve are given a garden, a life of abundance and stability and unbroken communion with God, but we know the story. They broke the communion and their sins broke them. They were expelled from the garden, and from then on, they lived as *wanderers*.

Many generations later, in search of stability, the nations came together and created political alliances. "They found a plain in Shinar and settled there" because "otherwise [they would] be *scattered* over the face of the whole earth" (Genesis 11:2, 4, emphasis added). They started building Babel, the greatest technological achievement of the day, "a city, with a tower that reaches to the heavens, so that [they] may make a name for [themselves]" (v. 4). They wanted to be their own little self-sustaining gods, and because of their obstinate hearts, "the LORD *scattered* them over the face of the whole earth" (v. 9, emphasis added). The early story of humankind is a story that feels like endless exile.

Turn to the very next chapter in Genesis and you find Abram and Sarai living lives of generational stability in Ur of the Chaldees. Abram is a seventy-five-year-old man enjoying his country, his people, and his father's household when Yahweh called them to "go . . . to the land I will show you" (12:1). So they packed their bags and left! They were promised a land for their descendants, but their descendants ended up living enslaved for some four hundred years in the land of Egypt. And after their exodus, they *wandered* in the wilderness for forty years before being settled in the promised land! And even after they got there, future generations of the people of God would be driven out to experience exile in Assyria, Babylon, and Persia. We could say that if God doesn't know how to be the God of all the wandering people, we're all in serious trouble.

But it turns out he knows what to do. And one of the preeminent Old Testament prophets spent a good deal of time teaching the people of God how to live when they're on the move, how to live when they find themselves in exile. He was Jeremiah of Anathoth. Most of us know one little sliver of this iconic passage found in the Hebrew scriptures:

> "For I know the plans I have for you," declares the LORD,
> "plans to prosper you and not to harm you, plans to give
> you hope and a future." (Jeremiah 29:11)

Many of us have these words from the Lord magnetized to our refrigerators, attached to our key chains, or hung on the walls of our living rooms: "For I know the plans I have for you." We give this verse to graduating high school seniors as an encouragement for the future. We pray these words over one another in church small groups that gather in homes around the city.

But for these words to crack with the force God intended, you have to know what came *before* these words. You have to know the first ten verses of chapter 29. You have to know to whom Jeremiah was *writing*. And you have to know what they were *going through*!

The chapter opens like this:

> This is the text of the letter that the prophet Jeremiah sent
> from Jerusalem to the surviving elders *among the exiles*
> and to the priests, the prophets and all the other people

Nebuchadnezzar had *carried into exile* from Jerusalem to Babylon. (Jeremiah 29:1, emphasis added)

He was writing to people who had been carried away from Jerusalem to Babylon. From Jerusalem, the holiest place in all the world for any Jew, the place where the eternal God dwelled, the place that had been their homeland for centuries. To Babylon, the homeland of their mortal enemies, the place of idolatry and impurity, the place that had now become their new home. And what did God say to his exiled and heartsick people through Jeremiah?

This is what the LORD Almighty, the God of Israel, says to all those I carried into exile from Jerusalem to Babylon: "Build houses and settle down; plant gardens and eat what they produce. Marry and have sons and daughters; find wives for your sons and give your daughters in marriage, so that they too may have sons and daughters. Increase in number there; do not decrease. Also, seek the peace and prosperity of the city to which I have carried you into exile. Pray to the LORD for it, because if it prospers, you too will prosper." Yes, this is what the LORD Almighty, the God of Israel, says: "Do not let the prophets and diviners among you deceive you. Do not listen to the dreams you encourage them to have. They are prophesying lies to you in my name. I have not sent them," declares the LORD.

This is what the LORD says: "When seventy years are completed for Babylon, I will come to you and fulfill my good promise to bring you back to this place." (vv. 4–10)

These words would have shot through the souls and the psyches of these dislocated saints. I can hear them pushing back in exasperation. "Build houses? Settle down? Plant gardens? Seek the peace and prosperity of this godforsaken and idolatrous place? And for *seventy years*? Are you *kidding me*? This isn't *us*! This isn't where we want to be! And this isn't the home you promised Father Abraham!"

They would have wrestled with these words from Jeremiah. It would have taken a while for the shock to wear off to hear it afresh: "Seek the peace and prosperity of the city to which I have carried you . . . because if it prospers, you too will prosper" (v. 7). But they eventually got around to living well in the land that wasn't their promised land.

Many of us have exactly the same thoughts when it becomes apparent that we're living in a place that doesn't feel like home, a place that probably won't be our final stop. It's easy just to mail it in, to check out, to do just enough to get by. I've talked to military families who have told me about showing up in a new town where they're going to be stationed for a mere twenty-four months, and how the day they arrive the countdown begins. They don't know where they'll be moving to, but they know that in two years they'll be moving again. It's a disorienting feeling, for sure. Many of them don't have the emotional energy to hang pictures on the walls of their rental home. Repainting walls into their own colors, the colors that bring them joy, often feels worthless.

In interviewing folks who have had to live lives of mobility, I've heard the questions they've had to wrestle with:

- Why would we invest the time and money and energy when we know we're leaving?
- Why would we really try to make good friends?
- Is it really worth getting involved in a local church? We could just have some Bible studies at home while we're here.

These are all very normal feelings and very understandable questions. These are the same questions asked by the people of God who were exiled in Babylon. But they pushed through and turned the place of exile into a fruitful land.

As I've talked to folks who've lived well while living on the move, some emerging themes have risen to the surface. They all pushed through the passivity and—to borrow Jeremiah's phrase—planted gardens that would bear fruit. They all worked to build friendships where they were. They invited people over for meals. The ones who had children helped their kids invest in local sports and they helped coach the team, an instant way of getting to know people. They encouraged their kids' involvement in school activities. The adults didn't retreat, and they didn't let their kids retreat either.

The ones who flourished had all gotten involved in local churches and made a commitment to attend weekly worship gatherings. They volunteered in the children's ministry or they helped park cars in the church parking lot or they agreed to be a chaperone at the junior high youth retreat. They introduced themselves to their pastors over lunch. They just kept showing up. And even though they were passing through, they thrived. They didn't live as strangers in a foreign land. They lived like the ancient people of God who figured out how to flourish in exile.

So if you're living a life that will require regular mobility, learn how to live well while you're passing through. Show up. Get involved. Do the hard work to plant gardens of relationship. Seek the peace and prosperity of the place you find yourself. And watch yourself thrive in a foreign land.

For God is the God who can cause abundance to spring up even in a land that feels like exile.

ACKNOWLEDGMENTS

MY NAME MAY BE ON THE COVER OF THIS BOOK, but anybody who has ever written a book knows that a book is never written alone. It is the result of a community of confidants and consultants and counselors.

To my friend and world-class literary agent, Alexander Field, and to all the fine people at the Bindery Literary Agency, thank you for representing me and helping me get this message farther afield. I'm deeply indebted to you.

To Erin Healy, your rigorous first round of edits and vision for what this book could be made it that much better. And to Jessica Wong Rogers and Sujin Hong, it was a pleasure working with you! You and your team at Nelson Books are consummate professionals.

To Pete Greig, Gyle Smith, Andrew Arndt, Glenn Packiam, Jon Egan, Rich Villodas, Jordan Prance, Dr. Ellen Davis, Kate Wyss, Kristi Garguile, Buz Hannon, Brett Davis, Chris Green, Winn Collier, and John Blase, thank you for your input and your willingness to help me refine my thoughts and crystallize these concepts.

To the Kings and Gowlers, my neighbors on Quiet Waters Ranch, I love you so much. And I thank God that we get to share our lives—and this land—together. Let's keep hallowing the ground that the Lord has given us.

To Wendell Berry, for your gracious correspondence around this project and your vigorous witness to stability over the decades, thank you. My life has been marked by you. And may your tribe increase.

To Pastor Brady Boyd and my family at New Life Church, thank you for making space for me to be planted and to grow up in the soil of this congregation. Being rooted here for nearly two decades has been one of the great delights of my life.

To my parents, David and Becky Grothe, and to my parents-in-law, Larry and Linda Wakley, you have been a daily example of the vow of stability. You'll never know how rich you've made me simply by living faithfully. I love you and bless you.

To my wife, Lisa, and to our three children, Lillian, Wilson, and Wakley—living the vow of stability *with you* is the great privilege of my life. I can sing it out with the psalmist: "The boundary lines have fallen for me in pleasant places." I love you with all my heart.

NOTES

Chapter 1: Wanderlust

1. Jonathan Wilson-Hartgrove, *The Wisdom of Stability: Rooting Faith in a Mobile Culture* (Brewster, MA: Paraclete Press, 2010), 37.

Chapter 2: The Vow of Stability

1. Rule of Saint Benedict, 1.10–11. https://www.gutenberg.org/files/50040/50040-0.txt.
2. Theology professor Gerald Schlabach of the University of Saint Thomas has written brilliantly on the Rule of Saint Benedict. See a thorough summary at Gerald W. Schlabach, "The Vow of Stability: A Premodern Way Through a Hypermodern World," n.d., https://www.geraldschlabach.net/the-vow-of-stability/#HX2.
3. Rule of Saint Benedict, 58:17.
4. American Psychological Association, "Moving Repeatedly in Childhood Associated with Poorer Quality of Life Years Later," June 4, 2010, https://www.apa.org/news/press/releases/2010/06/moving-well-being.
5. Shigehiro Oishi and Ulrich Schimmack, "Residential Mobility, Well-Being, and Mortality," *Journal of Personality and Social Psychology* 98, no. 6 (2010): 980–94, https://www.apa.org/pubs/journals/releases/psp-98-6-980.pdf.

6. American Psychological Association, "Moving Repeatedly in Childhood Associated with Poorer Quality of Life Years Later."

7. Jeffrey Bilbro, *Virtues of Renewal: Wendell Berry's Sustainable Forms* (Lexington: University Press of Kentucky, 2019), iii.

8. Shigehiro Oishi, "The Psychology of Residential Mobility: Implications for the Self, Social Relationships, and Well-Being," *Perspectives on Psychological Science 5*, no. 1 (January 2010).

9. Oishi, "Psychology of Residential Mobility."

10. John Inge, *A Christian Theology of Place* (Aldershot, UK: Ashgate, 2003), 130.

11. Bill Chappell, "U.K. Extends Coronavirus Furlough Payments to Workers Through End of October," NPR, May 12, 2020, https://www.npr.org/sections/coronavirus-live-updates/2020 /05/12/854459852/u-k-extends-coronavirus-job-furlough -program-through-end-of-october.

12. I first heard her explain this translation in an interview with Krista Tippett on NPR's *On Being* podcast. Tippett was one of Davis's former students. The interview is lively and lovely. See "Wendell Berry and Ellen Davis: The Art of Being Creatures," *On Being*, June 10, 2010, https://onbeing.org/programs /wendell-berry-ellen-davis-the-art-of-being-creatures/.

13. G. K. Chesterton, *Orthodoxy*, chapter 9, https://www .gutenberg.org/files/16769/16769-h/16769-h.htm #CHAPTER_IX_Authority_and_the_Adventurer.

Chapter 3: The Gift of Place

1. From "Wendell Berry and Ellen Davis: The Art of Being Creatures," *On Being*, June 10, 2010, https://onbeing.org /programs/wendell-berry-ellen-davis-the-art-of-being-creatures/.

2. A perspective that first became apparent to me after listening to Ellen Davis's interview with Krista Tippett; see "Wendell

Berry and Ellen Davis: The Art of Being Creatures," *On Being*, June 10, 2010, https://onbeing.org/programs /wendell-berry-ellen-davis-the-art-of-being-creatures/.

3. Eugene H. Peterson, *Christ Plays in Ten Thousand Places: A Conversation in Spiritual Theology* (Grand Rapids, MI: Eerdmans, 2005), 76.

Chapter 4: Honoring Your Location

1. N. T. Wright, *The Day the Revolution Began: Reconsidering the Meaning of Jesus's Crucifixion* (San Francisco: HarperOne, 2016).

2. Norman Wirzba, ed., *The Art of the Commonplace: The Agrarian Essays of Wendell Berry* (Washington, DC: Shoemaker and Hoard, 2002).

3. Wendell Berry, *The Unsettling of America: Culture & Agriculture*, rev. ed. (Washington, DC: Counterpoint, 1996), Kindle loc. 2347–48.

4. Wendell Berry, "Sabbaths—1979, IV," from *The Selected Poems of Wendell Berry* (Washington, DC: Counterpoint, 1998), https://onbeing.org/poetry/sabbaths-1979-iv/.

5. Mary Oliver, *Upstream: Select Essays* (New York: Penguin, 2016).

6. Wendell Berry, "How to Be a Poet (to Remind Myself)," from *The Selected Poems of Wendell Berry* (Washington, DC: Counterpoint, 1998), https://onbeing.org/blog/parker -palmer-how-to-be-a-poet/.

7. Jason Peters, "From the Editor—The Inaugural Issue of Local Culture," Front Porch Republic, September 11, 2019, https:// www.frontporchrepublic.com/2019/09/from-the-editor-the -inaugural-issue-of-local-culture/.

8. Donald Hall, "Back to the Land," review of *The Unsettling of America* by Wendell Berry, *New York Times*, September 25, 1977, https://www.nytimes.com/1977/09/25/archives /back-to-the-land.html.

9. Burley Coulter, quoted in Wendell Berry, *The Wild Birds: Six Stories of the Port William Membership* (Berkeley, CA: Counterpoint, 2019).

10. Berry, *Unsettling of America*, Kindle loc. 312–13.

11. James Gallagher, "'Global Epidemic' of Childhood Inactivity," BBC News, November 22, 2019, https://www .bbc.com/news/health-50466061#:~:text=Four%20in %20five%2011%2D%20to,brain%20development %20and%20social%20skills.

Chapter 5: Honoring Your Relationships

1. Thomas Merton, *The Sign of Jonas* (New York: Harcourt, Brace, 1953).

2. "Vows," Our Lady of the Mississippi Abbey, https://www .mississippiabbey.org/vows.

Chapter 6: Honoring Your Service

1. Kevin Sullivan and Mary Jordan, "The Un-Celebrity President: Jimmy Carter Shuns Riches, Lives Modestly in His Georgia Hometown," *Washington Post*, August 17, 2018, https://www.washingtonpost.com/news/national /wp/2018/08/17/feature/the-un-celebrity-president-jimmy -carter-shuns-riches-lives-modestly-in-his-georgia -hometown/.

2. Robert A. Strong, "Jimmy Carter: Life Before the Presidency," University of Virginia, Miller Center, n.d., https://millercenter .org/president/carter/life-before-the-presidency.

3. Eugene H. Peterson, *A Long Obedience in the Same Direction: Discipleship in an Instant Society* (Westmont, IL: InterVarsity Press, 2021).

4. Miranda Siwak, "Jimmy and Rosalynn Carter Have a Love Story for the Ages," *Good Housekeeping*, July 20, 2017, https://www.goodhousekeeping.com/life/relationships /a45118/jimmy-and-roslynn-carter-love-story/.

5. Siwak, "Jimmy and Rosalynn Carter Have a Love Story for the Ages."
6. Siwak, "Jimmy and Rosalynn Carter Have a Love Story for the Ages."
7. Sullivan and Jordan, "The Un-Celebrity President."
8. Strong, "Jimmy Carter: Life Before the Presidency."
9. Strong, "Jimmy Carter: Life Before the Presidency."
10. "The Nobel Peace Prize for 2002," Nobel Prize, Nobel Media AB 2021, https://www.nobelprize.org/prizes/peace/2002/press-release/.
11. Strong, "Jimmy Carter: Life Before the Presidency."
12. Sullivan and Jordan, "The Un-Celebrity President."
13. Frederick Buechner, *Wishful Thinking: A Theological ABC* (New York: Harper & Row, 1973).
14. The phrase "The world is charged with the grandeur of God. . . . It gathers to a greatness" comes from Gerard Manley Hopkins, "God's Grandeur" (1877), Poetry Foundation, https://www.poetryfoundation.org/poems/44395/gods-grandeur.

Chapter 7: Honoring Your Presence

1. Flannery O'Connor coined the term *Christ-haunted* in her essay "Southern Fiction," in *Mystery and Manners: Occasional Prose, Selected and Edited by Sally and Robert Fitzgerald* (New York: Farrar, Straus & Giroux, 1969), 44: "I think it is safe to say that while the South is hardly Christ-centered, it is most certainly Christ-haunted."
2. Bob Richardson, "Biography of Annie Dillard by Bob Richardson," Annie Dillard Official Website, n.d., http://www.anniedillard.com/biography-by-bob-richardson.html.
3. Paul Roberts, review of *For the Time Being* by Annie Dillard, *Toronto Globe and Mail*, n.d., quoted in Richardson, "Biography of Annie Dillard," http://www.anniedillard.com/biography-by-bob-richardson.html.

4. Diana Saverin, "The Thoreau of the Suburbs," *Atlantic*, February 5, 2015, https://www.theatlantic.com/culture /archive/2015/02/the-thoreau-of-the-suburbs/385128/.

5. Mary Cantwell, "A Pilgrim's Progress," review of *Pilgrim at Tinker Creek* by Annie Dillard, *New York Times*, April 26, 1992, https://archive.nytimes.com/www.nytimes.com/books /99/03/28/specials/dillard-pilgrim.html.

6. Saverin, "The Thoreau of the Suburbs."

7. Annie Dillard, *Holy the Firm* (New York: Harper & Row, 1977), 17.

8. Doris Grumbach, literary editor of the *New Republic*, quoted on the front cover of Annie Dillard, *Pilgrim at Tinker Creek* (New York: Harper's Magazine Press, 1974).

9. Cantwell, "A Pilgrim's Progress."

10. See Strong's 37; or Joseph Henry Thayer, Carl Ludwig Wilibald Grimm, and Christian Gottlob Wilke, *A Greek-English Lexicon of the New Testament: Being Grimm's Wilke's Clavis Novi Testamenti* (New York: American Book Co., 1889), s.v. "hallowed."

11. Henry David Thoreau, *Walden, or Life in the Woods* (Boston: Ticknor and Fields, 1854), 178.

12. Annie Dillard, *Pilgrim at Tinker Creek*, Modern Classics Edition (New York: Harper Perennial, 2007), 10.

13. George Arthur Buttrick, quoted in Richard L. Morgan, *Autumn Wisdom: A Book of Readings* (Nashville: Upper Room, 1995), 44.

14. Susan Elizabeth Yore, "The Mystic Way in Postmodernity: Transcending Theological Boundaries in the Writings of Iris Murdoch, Denise Levertov and Annie Dillard," PhD diss., Durham University, 2006, http://etheses.dur.ac.uk/1810/.

Chapter 8: Stability in Home

1. Wendell Berry coined the phrase in *The Unsettling of America* (1977).

2. Jeffrey Bilbro, *Virtues of Renewal: Wendell Berry's Sustainable Forms* (Lexington: University Press of Kentucky, 2019), introduction.

Chapter 9: Stability in Family

1. Toni Morrison, "The Work You Do, the Person You Are," *New Yorker*, May 29, 2017, https://www.newyorker.com /magazine/2017/06/05/the-work-you-do-the-person-you-are.
2. Morrison, "The Work You Do, the Person You Are."
3. Morrison, "The Work You Do, the Person You Are."
4. The phrase "consciously uncouple" was coined in 2009 by Katherine Woodward Thomas, and it was made famous in 2014 when actress Gwyneth Paltrow and rock star Chris Martin announced their divorce this way.
5. Habib Sadeghi and Sherry Sami, "Conscious Uncoupling," Goop, n.d., https://goop.com/wellness/relationships /conscious-uncoupling-2/.
6. Sadeghi and Sami, "Conscious Uncoupling."
7. John Chrysostom, Homily 20 on Ephesians 5:22–33, from Philip Schaff, *Nicene and Post-Nicene Fathers*, 1st ser., vol. 13, trans. Gross Alexander, rev. and ed. Kevin Knight (Buffalo, NY: Christian Literature Publishing Co., 1889), http://www.newadvent.org/fathers/230120.htm.
8. John M. Gottman and Nan Silver, *The Seven Principles for Making Marriage Work* (New York: Crown, 1999).
9. Stanley Hauerwas, "Sex and Politics: Bertrand Russell and 'Human Sexuality,'" *Christian Century*, April 19, 1978, 417–22.
10. Wendell Berry, "How to Be a Poet (to Remind Myself)," from *The Selected Poems of Wendell Berry* (Washington, DC: Counterpoint, 1998), https://onbeing.org/blog/parker -palmer-how-to-be-a-poet/.
11. Dante Alighieri, *The Divine Comedy* (United Kingdom: J. Wisotzki, 1891).

Chapter 10: Stability in Friendship

1. Arthur C. Brooks, "How Loneliness Is Tearing America Apart," *New York Times*, November 23, 2018, https://www.nytimes.com/2018/11/23/opinion/loneliness-political-polarization.html?fbclid=IwAR1DiDMBerFX7fR9-PiCQfGEhBLbJnLU-yhloJewgrRRI2IRuZEdPVFeG10. In the article, Brooks addresses the transient gig economy and the resulting loneliness of Americans.

2. Dallas Willard, *Hearing God: Developing a Conversational Relationship with God* (Westmont, IL: InterVarsity Press, 2012).

3. "Proceeds from the Father and the Son" is a phrase in the church's oldest creed, the Nicene Creed, written in AD 325.

Chapter 11: Stability in Church

1. Thomas à Kempis, *Imitation of Christ*, quoted in Neil Young, "Ancient Voices: Why I Prefer Wisdom from the Elders Rather than the Youngers," *Christianity Today*, Spring 2006, https://www.christianitytoday.com/pastors/2006/spring/14.73.html.

2. Charles H. Kraft, *I Give You Authority: Practicing the Authority Jesus Gave Us*, rev. ed. (Minneapolis: Chosen, 2012), 291–93.

3. "Episode 035: A Conversation with Louie Giglio," August 28, 2018, *Essential Church* podcast, 00:15, https://theessential.church/episode-035-a-conversation-with-louie-giglio/.

4. "Episode 035: A Conversation with Louie Giglio."

5. Billy Graham Evangelistic Association Staff, "Notable Quotes from Billy Graham: On Regrets," Billy Graham Evangelistic Association, November 5, 2009, https://billygraham.org/story/notable-quotes-from-billy-graham/.

6. Kraft, *I Give You Authority*, 291–93.

Chapter 12: Stability in Community

1. Eugene H. Peterson, *Reversed Thunder: The Revelation of John and the Praying Imagination* (San Francisco: Harper & Row, 1988), 56.

Chapter 13: A Sacred Stay

1. Marilynne Robinson, *The Death of Adam: Essays on Modern Thought* (Boston: Houghton Mifflin, 1998), 235.

ABOUT THE AUTHOR

DANIEL GROTHE IS THE ASSOCIATE SENIOR PASTOR at New Life Church in Colorado Springs, Colorado, where he's been for sixteen years. Daniel and his wife, Lisa, live on a hobby farm outside of Colorado Springs with their three children—Lillian, Wilson, Wakley—and a thriving throng of happy animals.